The Ultimate IRS Survival Guide

James Harnsberger, EA

Copyright © 2017 James Harnsberger, EA

All rights reserved.

ISBN-10:1973863243
ISBN-13: 978-1973863243

DEDICATION

This book is dedicated to my beautiful wife, Susan and to all that makes her a wonderful human being.

CONTENTS

	Acknowledgments	i
1	Death & Taxes	3
2	Taxes & Secret Self Sabotage	11
3	Don't Bury your head in the sand	22
4	Knowing your tax problem	36
5	There's a Bloodbath Coming	44
6	Games the IRS Plays	62
7	Knowing your Real Rights	70
8	Never do these things	77
9	The EXACT steps to protect yourself	85
10	What's next for you	92

ACKNOWLEDGMENTS

I would like to acknowledge Richard Vermazen, Esq. for the great opportunity to learn so much from him, and for his wisdom and character to mentor me. Also to all the many clients who I have had the honor to represent in matters before the IRS and where we were successful at resolving and in many cases eliminating the tax problems that nearly devastated their lives

Chapter 1
Death and Taxes

- Some people may feel taxes to be unconstitutional and unfair, but it doesn't matter

First is you take the position taxes are unconstitutional you will need a good criminal attorney not this e-book! That argument will land you straight in federal prison; just ask Wesley Snipes!

The law is very clear and if you refuse or fail to file your taxes or pay your tax obligations you will run afoul of the law and will be dealing with the IRS enforcement system. You are required to file a tax return to report all income regardless of how you earn it or where you earn it. Even if you are in a foreign country earning money and are a US citizen you must file a tax return on time (April 15) each year.

The failure to file a tax return can and will lead to civil penalties and could be potentially a criminal case resulting in you doing jail time, and having to pay restitution to the government for the cost to prosecute you. If you have any doubt about the IRS referring you for criminal prosecution simply check it out on the IRS website.

Bottom line if you earn money of any kind you must file a tax return each year and if you owe taxes you must pay them. Each year it is estimated 12,000,000 million taxpayers do not file their tax returns; and IRS has sophisticated automated enforcement tools to track you down and send you a notice to file that return. This filing enforcement action is generally the first step into an area where it can become very tricky on how you resolve the problem.

Anatomy of a Tax Problem

There are two primary tax problems that millions of people find themselves facing every year. First more than 12 Million people who fail to file a tax return EACH YEAR and second, Millions more that fail to pay their taxes every year. When you do not file and pay your taxes you enter this twilight zone of mystery, fear, confusion, denial and even self destruction because it never stops with a single tax year or ends with a single payment.

It begins rather simply in fact; you make some money; life gets in the way and next thing you know April 15 comes and goes and Ooops you forgot to file; or simply ignored filing. This grows into a problem that gets more serious every year because once you hit that first year of not filing or paying now you work yourself into a frenzy trying to ignore it and decide you deal with it later when you have more time, more money, more whatever!

You also likely have little or no records, perhaps you did not receive a 1099 and think you have no obligation but deep down you know you have not filed or paid your taxes and you know you are required to file and pay your taxes so you find simple ways to make excuses to yourself and justify not doing anything about it.

Here is the truth

You make any money from any source whatsoever worldwide you MUST file a tax return and PAY any tax you owe PERIOD!

- They are one of the few certainties in life

The old adage is *"the only thing certain in life is death and taxes"* Well taxes are truly certain and the government wants their money from you in the form of taxes you owe on all sources of income you make. When you have a business it is even more serious when you do not file or pay your taxes. When you die you may actually owe estate taxes upon your death. Just to list a few taxes you should be aware of; income taxes, self employment taxes, alternative minimum taxes, capital gains tax, unemployment tax, employment taxes, FICA, Medicare, estate taxes, excise taxes on gasoline, oil, road excise taxes and on and on and on….. Taxes are the source of money that pay for a HUGE AND GROWING

GOVERNMENT and it is HUNGRY and wants to be fed everyday!

Think about the fact that when you earn money on a paycheck and look at the gross then the net; the difference between these two numbers is all the TAX you pay withheld from your paycheck! When you earn money in your business someone pays you for something, you pay expenses for the business then the profits are subject to tax! Income tax and self employment tax at a minimum!

If you make too much money you then get to pay additional taxes such as alternative minimum tax, or an additional Medicare tax or you lose valuable deductions because you made too much money which is in effect a new tax!

Here is the real problem....hardly any business owner or taxpayer understands, knows or could name three taxes they are subject to and forget having them explain anything on the tax return!

- Brief history of the IRS and its role

Origin of the IRS

The roots of IRS go back to the Civil War when President Lincoln and Congress, in 1862, created the position of commissioner of Internal Revenue and enacted an income tax to pay war expenses. The income tax was repealed 10 years later. Congress revived the income tax in 1894, but the Supreme Court ruled it unconstitutional the following year.

16th Amendment

In 1913, Wyoming ratified the 16th Amendment, providing the three-quarter majority of states necessary to amend the Constitution. The 16th Amendment gave Congress the authority to enact an income tax. That same year, the first Form 1040 appeared after Congress levied a 1 percent tax on net personal incomes above $3,000 with a 6 percent surtax on incomes of more than $500,000.

In 1918, during World War I, the top rate of the income tax rose to 77 percent to help finance the war effort. It dropped sharply in the post-war years, down to 24 percent in 1929, and rose again during the Depression. During World War II, Congress introduced payroll withholding and quarterly tax payments.

1913 Form 1040 (PDF 126KB, 4 pages, including instructions)

A New Name

In the 50s, the agency was reorganized to replace a patronage system with career, professional employees. The Bureau of Internal Revenue name was changed to the Internal Revenue Service. Only the IRS commissioner and chief counsel are selected by the president and confirmed by the Senate.

Today's IRS Organization

The IRS Restructuring and Reform Act of 1998 prompted the most comprehensive reorganization and modernization of IRS in nearly half a century. The IRS reorganized itself to closely resemble the private sector model of organizing around customers with similar needs. The IRS actually refers to you as a customer but trust me, you are anything but a customer!

- They are not your friend, they want you to pay and as soon as possible or else!

The IRS is not in the business to be your friend or companion! They are an agency of the federal government; they have police powers, they can confiscate your property and assets through a seizure, they can lien you and your property, they can confiscate all the money on your bank account, retirement account, social security benefits, pension money, they can seize your car, your business, your tools and equipment....in short they can and will make your life miserable if you do not file your tax returns or pay your taxes. Finally they can throw you in jail! Federal prison and lock you up for years for tax evasion!

You could have a Revenue Officer or Criminal Investigation Special Agent visit you at your home, your office, talk to your neighbors, follow you on Facebook, and when you least expect it drop the hammer on you and BAM! You are now is serious trouble!

Criminal Investigation's (CI) primary commitment is to develop and investigate Legal Source Tax Crimes. The prosecution of these cases is key to supporting the IRS and its overall compliance goals, enhancing voluntary compliance with the tax laws, and promoting fairness and equity in our tax system. Legal Source Tax investigations involve taxpayers in legal industries and legal occupations, who earned income legally, but choose to evade taxes by violation of tax laws. Not filing tax returns or cheating on the returns they file!

The Legal Source Tax Crimes Program includes those cases that threaten the tax system, such as the Questionable Refund Program (QRP) cases, unscrupulous return preparers and frivolous filers/non-filers who challenge the legality of the filing requirement. Additional important elements of the program are excise tax and employment tax investigations. This Program emphasizes the importance of cooperation between Service compliance functions as well as with Chief Counsel's Office and Department of Justice Tax Division.

Each level of review may determine that evidence does not substantiate criminal charges and the investigation should not be prosecuted.

Prosecution

If the Department of Justice or the United States Attorney accepts the investigation for prosecution, the IRS special agent will be asked by the prosecutors to assist in preparation for trial. However, once a special agent report is referred to for prosecution, the investigation is managed by the prosecutors.

Conviction

The ultimate goal of an IRS Criminal Investigation prosecution recommendation is to obtain a conviction - either by a guilty verdict or plea. Approximately 3,000 criminal prosecutions per year provide a deterrent effect and signals to our compliant taxpayers that fraud will not be tolerated.

When you do not file on time you get hit with penalties or possible federal prison

Not Filing and Not Paying Are Not the Same

This belief is a very serious mistake, because the IRS penalizes for both not filing and not paying. So, what can you do if you calculate your return only to realize you don't have the money to pay the tax? Many people in this situation believe they shouldn't file if they don't have the money. Again, it would be a big mistake not to pay. But, why?

Well, you end up paying a penalty on the amount you owe at 5% per month (4.5 % for not filing and 0.5% for not paying). The total penalty for failure to file and pay can eventually add up to 47.5% (22.5% late filing, 25% late payment) of the tax owed. Interest, compounded daily, is also charged on any unpaid tax from the due date of the return until the date of payment.
The point is that failing to file a tax return should never be an option.

What if you fail to file?

The IRS may file what is known as a substitute return for you. However, as you well know, the IRS will not be looking to save you any money. In fact, a substitute return will not include any of the standard deductions you would typically include in your return. Case in point, a substitute return only allows one exemption: single or married filing separate, so you end up with higher tax liability than if you would have just filed.

Then they assess the tax and penalties add the interest and BAM you are in deep waters owing the IRS because you did not file and they filed for you. Now they can begin to collect the tax you owe based on what they filed for you and start enforcement action to collect!

- You are not a person to them, just a number on a screen

You have a Social Security Number referred to as a TIN (taxpayer identification number) if you have a business you likely have an EFIN (Employer Federal Identification Number) and the IRS does not care about your spouse, your kids, your dog butch or how nice you are! All they care about is where is your tax return and the money you owe!!!!
They deal with millions of tax returns daily and millions of taxpayers (You) every hour and they have no time or patience for excuses! They want a tax return and the money you owe and they want it now.

You literally are nothing but a number in the system. And the IRS has dozens of computer files on you; Your master file, your account transcript records, your Business Master File, and they may even have an open investigation file on you for non filing of your return where they are gathering evidence as you sleep so they can hit you with that Hammer for not filing your number.
They can track you back to a bank account, cross reference to your vehicle registration, home, insurance policies; they have more information on you under your number that you could ever imagine! And they are now coming after you if you have not filed your returns!
Some Examples of the many computer files the IRS maintains on you

TXMOD files
IMF files
BMF files

IRP files
IDRS files
ERCS files
AIMS files
AMIR files
EIRS files

These are but a few of the hundreds of computer file codes the IRS has that keep track of you and what information the IRS has on you.

Chapter 2
Taxes and Secret Self-Sabotage

- If you've been ignoring a tax problem, I've got news for you...

Once you reach one tax year where you do not file a return or pay your taxes it is very likely you will repeat this pattern a few more years. You get scared, anxious and uncertain because you are unsure how to resolve it and how to deal with the IRS. SO you do like 12 million other people do every year, you ignore it and hope somehow it will not turn into a problem before you find a way to get it resolved. You likely think to yourself that the next big bonus check you will take time and get caught up, but somehow you never get around to resolving it.

I have news for you…..The IRS will NOT ignore it. Your tax ID number will be flagged automatically as not having filed a tax return. Eventually the automated computer system will get around to you and if it is within certain criteria your case will be referred to a Revenue Officer or worse a IRS Special Agent (they carry guns and wear a badge).

I guarantee you the IRS knows you have not filed a tax return and I also guarantee you that it is not IF but WHEN they finally work through the other millions of people and get around to you. The world of technology is great but it has another side; that same technology is now allowing IRS to track you down, locate you and your assets, follow you on Facebook, and locate all your assets before dropping the hammer on you.

Ignoring it will eventually be a decision that could result in your situation becoming one of a more serious tax issue, perhaps even criminal. This sabotage also takes a toll on you emotionally; you worry and have stress, you know you have a problem but try to stay quietly in the state of denial and this sabotages your success and your ability to do so many other things that could be great success stories for you except that you have this issue of not filing your tax returns for five years now and you are really worried about HOW MUCH YOU WILL OWE when you finally come clean!

- You've been limiting, even sabotaging your wealth potential in ways you can't imagine

Once you are in the camp of two or more years you worry about setting up a bank account, you use your spouse or friend to manage your merchant account and this places limits on your ability to operate a business or enjoy your life without walking around everyday looking over your shoulder.

This takes a huge toll in that you are not operating at optimum levels because you are worried when that knock on the door will come or that notice from the IRS arrive in your mailbox. You spend so much time managing ways to stay off the radar not realizing that the IRS is working hard to use technology to track you down like a dog and compel you to file your taxes and pay your bill to the HUGE federal government! How can you ever accumulate wealth when you worry about all of this and have to worry the IRS will take it all away from you!

- It may seem like you're holding onto the extra money and you're getting "more"

When you earn money in your business what you may not realize is the IRS is your partner! For every dollar you earn you owe the IRS 25% maybe even 40% in various taxes if you have no plan and have no way to manage these issues!

You might be thinking all that money is yours but the real truth is you really do know you owe something to the IRS for the money you make; you might just think that because they haven't caught up with you so far that you're okay! WRONG!

You are required to pay estimated taxes every quarter on the money you earn. You must send it in to the IRS for your estimated tax payments. If you fail to do that you will have civil penalties;

failure to file, failure to pay estimated taxes, underpayment of taxes, late filing penalty and again possible criminal prosecution for tax evasion!

Income Tax

All businesses except partnerships must file an annual income tax return. Partnerships file an information return. The form you use depends on how your business is organized.

The federal income tax is a pay-as-you-go tax. You must pay the tax as you earn or receive income during the year. An employee usually has income tax withheld from his or her pay. If you do not pay your tax through withholding, or do not pay enough tax that way, you might have to pay estimated tax. If you are not required to make estimated tax payments, you may pay any tax due when you file your return.

Estimated tax

Generally, you must pay taxes on income, including self-employment tax (discussed next), by making regular payments of estimated tax during the year.

Self-Employment Tax

Self-employment tax (SE tax) is a social security and Medicare tax primarily for individuals who work for themselves. Your payments of SE tax contribute to your coverage under the social security system. Social security coverage provides you with retirement benefits, disability benefits, survivor benefits, and hospital insurance (Medicare) benefits.

Generally, you must pay SE tax and file Schedule SE (Form 1040) if either of the following applies.

If your net earnings from self-employment were $400 or more. If you work for a church or a qualified church-controlled organization (other than as a minister or member of a religious order) that elected an exemption from social security and Medicare taxes, you are subject to SE tax if you receive $108.28 or more in wages from the church or organization. There are Special Rules and Exceptions for aliens, fishing crew members, notary public, State or local government employees, foreign government or international organization employees, etc. For additional information, refer to Self-Employment Tax.

Employment Taxes

When you have employees, you as the employer have certain employment tax responsibilities that you must pay and forms you must file. Employment taxes include the following:
Social security and Medicare taxes
Federal income tax withholding
Federal unemployment (FUTA) tax

Excise Tax

The following describes the excise taxes you may have to pay and the forms you have to file if you do any of the following.

Manufacture or sell certain products.
Operate certain kinds of businesses.
Use various kinds of equipment, facilities, or products.
Receive payment for certain services.
Form 720 - The federal excise taxes reported on Form 720, consist of several broad categories of taxes, including the following.

- But the reality is you're building debt and unconscious barrier toward financial freedom, security and abundance

Every day you delay you risk filing or collection enforcement action! Every day you delay you risk getting nailed and you build the wall higher against your having wealth, financial freedom, and security and peace of mind!

Wealthy people are wealthy for many reasons and one of them includes managing their money and taxes!

Wealth is about accumulating and preserving assets and when you have tax problems it is impossible to build wealth on any level. The civil penalties alone can add 75% of the total tax to your bill for civil penalties PLUS interest; in effect you could more than double what you owe by ignoring filing and paying your taxes. In the back of your mind you stay in that state of denial thinking that if you can just get to the next whatever.... You will get it resolved.

Once you have a situation where you have two or more years of non filed returns and unpaid taxes you really have a case where you need to confront the issues and begin dealing with how you are going to begin solving this problem before it ends up in enforcement action or worse a criminal case against you.

How can you run and grow a business with no financial stability and no tax returns? How can you build that business and focus on what is important to grow the busness when you are worrie everyday that the IRS may contact you?
The real solution is simple....you have to come to a decision once and for all that you are going to take care of this problem, find out what you need to do to file the returns and or pay the taxes you may owe. The irony is that many people really can solve these smaller cases in a Do-It-Yourself manner if they knew the process and some of the basic procedures and how to go about filling out the various forms.

Non Filed Returns

Did the IRS file an SFR return? If yes you need to file an original return to substitute the SFR return IRS filed for you. Sometimes this may involve having to file an appeal because the IRS will file the return for you then conduct an audit of that return THEY prepared for you then hit you with the penalties, taxes, interest and assessments then you have to appeal the audit they did on the return they prepared!!!! So much for being a customer!

A non filed return case always involves two parts; non filing of returns and payment of the taxes once filed. So you have filing enforcement and collection enforcement both of which could require appeals of previous actions before you can get back on track. This becomes overwhelming even for the most patient of people because if you have no experience in these areas you become paralyzed into non action.

Filed Returns with unpaid balance due

Here tax returns were filed but you owe taxes, interest and penalties. This becomes a collection enforcement case and depending upon the total amount you owe the procedures and rules are very different.

$25,000 total tax and lower   No problem
IRS will grant installment agreement

$25,001 up to $50,000   Problem
You need to provide financial disclosure

$50,001 and up   Problem
You need to provide extensive financial disclosure

You must know the TOTAL of all amounts you owe the IRS before you begin this process. How you get that amount is order your account transcripts for all tax years to see if there is a balance due and how much. You do this using IRS Form 4506T to order transcripts!

What if you don't file voluntarily

Substitute Return

If you fail to file, IRS may file a substitute return for you. This return might not give you credit for deductions and exemptions you may be entitled to receive. IRS will send you a Notice of Deficiency CP3219N (90-day letter) proposing a tax assessment. You will have 90 days to file your past due tax return or file a petition in Tax Court. If you do neither, IRS will proceed with a proposed assessment. If you have received notice <u>CP3219N</u> you cannot request an extension to file.

If any of the income listed is incorrect, you may do the following:
Contact IRS at 1-866-681-4271 to let them know.
Contact the payer (source) of the income to request a corrected Form W-2 or 1099.
Attach the corrected forms when you send us your completed tax returns.

If the IRS files a substitute return, it is still in your best interest to file your own tax return to take advantage of any exemptions, credits and deductions you are entitled to receive. The IRS will generally adjust your account to reflect the correct figures.

Collection and enforcement actions

The return IRS prepares for you (the proposed assessment) will lead to a tax bill, which, if unpaid, will trigger the collection process. This can include such actions as a levy on your wages or bank account or the filing of a notice of federal tax lien.

If you repeatedly do not file, you could be subject to additional enforcement measures, such as additional penalties and/or criminal prosecution and prison time.

- My goal with this book and any of my programs and services is to help liberate your full earning power

You CANNOT reach your financial potential until you resolve your tax problems and begin to improve your relationship with your money!

I want you to succeed!
I want you to be filthy rich!
I want you to have freedom financially!

The problem is I cannot do any of what I want until you want to solve your problems! You liberate your earning power by controlling your money including your taxes. You start there by filing on time and paying what you owe on time!

Step 1   How big is your problem
Step 2   What is the game plan to begin solving your problem
Step 3   When do you start to solve the problem

Like any problem you have to first accept and admit there is a problem. If you are not filing or paying your taxes, you have a problem. How big it is depends on how many years and how much money you owe. You want to have some ability to file those older returns you did not file but you may have fear keeping you from taking that first step!!

At the end of the day I promise you as bad as you may think that is it is NOTHING compared to ignoring it and having the IRS show up and grab you!

I want to help you gain control of your taxes and solve your problem by encouraging you and giving you hope. I have helped resolve hundreds of cases over the years, some of which were in the near MILLIONS or more the client owed! They were all solved eventually but at the end of the day it could not have been solved until the client decided it was time to end the nightmare and get it solved!

- On the surface this is about solving your tax problem; helping you save tens of thousands or even hundreds of thousands of dollars and avoid jail is a big part of that

My DIY program will guide you through the steps depending on what your problem is and give you each step and what you need to do to begin solving your problems with the IRS. More important than that is the value you receive when you regain control of your money and begin to live a stress free life so that you can actually accumulate wealth!

You are not using tax strategies that could save you hundreds even thousands of dollars in tax because you have not filed a return or paid your taxes!

You cannot save that money if you are in trouble with the IRS. You may have formed an LLC to hide behind that because you do not want the IRS to know where you are. SO you form it in Nevada not knowing the IRS already knows where you are it is simply a matter of time before they get around to dealing with you. They have all the time in the world.

When you do not file a return and the IRS files it for you there is NO statute of limitations on the time the IRS can come after you to collect the tax!!!! In 20 years with that tax lien your $25000 tax bill turns into $450,000 and you cannot buy a home, retire, or do anything because the IRS was here before you were born and will be here after you die! They have all the time in the world and can screw with your financial life in so many ways now with technology.

- But on a deeper level, this is about transforming your relationship with your money, ending a pattern that as it's fixed, will help you experience your fullest potential for financial freedom and happiness

Admit it! Your relationship with your money SUCKS!

Not filing returns!
Not paying your taxes!
No retirement planning!
No financial Planning!
No business planning!

Really! Do you really want to live like this? NO!

You have to want to transform your relationship with your money and you have to want to put this nightmare behind you! You simply do not know where to begin. What we need is to break down the problem, define where you fit in the various types of problems and then start mapping out a plan to SOLVE YOUR problem!

How can you ever reach your fullest potential if all your life you run and hide!
You are a business owner, an American! We don't run and hide! We fight and we keep fighting until we WIN!

Believe it or not I have had clients who were so lucky not having filed tax returns for 8, 9 even 13 years in one recent case! Once they accepted there was no alternative but to suck it up and get in there and get it done, it was as if their entire life transformed right before my eyes!
The relief they felt, the feeling of finally getting it solved and the hope that they could now move forward and build a business, a retirement plan and accumulate wealth or whatever they desired was truly now an option!

Transforming your relationship with your money is much about accepting the reality of your circumstances and taking responsibility to improve them. That process when you have tax problems begins with defining the type of problem, non filed or unpaid taxes and educating yourself about what it will take to turn it around.

Then the next steps involve you taking one step forward, and begin to organize the problem into smaller more manageable size tasks, learn the process and procedure for each step and then work a little each day forward to until you complete each step as you move to the next.

Finally the process of transformation is to take steps to stop repeating what led to you getting behind in the first place. Stop ignoring your taxes, your filing requirements and making estimated tax payments going forward so you no longer continue digging the hole deeper each passing month. Be involved and engaged in your money, your taxes and your responsibility to stay current. Setting realistic goals, and manage them daily if necessary and soon you will find that you actually worry less, enjoy business and life more and you actually learn more about your money and thus improve your relationship with it.

It is not about how much you make as it is how much you keep and if you do not file and pay your taxes and end up paying over half or 75% to taxes, interest and penalties how could you ever expect to have financial freedom while at the same time risking prison or bankruptcy or ruined credit with dozens of tax liens filed against you.

Chapter 3
Don't Bury Your Head in the Sand

- When your taxes aren't taken out, it's easy to ignore them

When you make money and collect it through your merchant processing system or however it is you are actually paid it is very easy to think that is all your money. However, we all know that is not true and we also know that we have to report that money regardless if we receive a 1099 or not and we also know we owe something on taxes for what we earned.

It is very easy to bury your head in the sand and pretend it is not a problem in fact it is so easy we convince ourselves that if we do not get a 1099 the IRS knows nothing so therefore I will take my chances and odds are I will not get caught. I can introduce you to hundreds of people who thought the very same thing. After their prison sentence and parole was over, I think they would say to you how crazy it is to think in such terms as that. They too thought the very same things and it got each of them between 28 months and 90 months in a federal prison with civil penalties and criminal restitution owed to the IRS in the hundreds of thousands of dollars.

The only way to assure you do not build a snowball big enough to bury you in tax debt is to manage it every month a little at a time. Pay your estimates on time and on a regular basis. DO not depend on others to do what is your responsibility. After all it is you who will be fined or even prosecuted when you fail to file or pay your taxes. And to be perfectly honest you really know deep down inside that you owe something, you just prefer to pretend that if you do not see it then it must not exist.

Estimated tax is the method used to pay tax on income that is not subject to withholding. This includes income from self-employment, interest, dividends, alimony, rent, gains from the sale of assets, prizes and awards. You also may have to pay estimated tax if the amount of income tax being withheld from your salary, pension, or other income is not enough.

Estimated tax is used to pay income tax and self-employment tax, as well as other taxes and amounts reported on your tax return. If you do not pay enough through withholding or estimated tax payments, you may be charged a penalty. If you do not pay enough by the due date of each payment period you may be charged a penalty even if you are due a refund when you file your tax return.

How to Pay Estimated Tax

If you are filing as a sole proprietor, partner, S corporation shareholder and/or a self-employed individual, you should use Form 1040-ES, Estimated Tax for Individuals (PDF), to figure and pay your estimated tax. For specific information on how to pay online, by phone, or by mail, refer to the section of Form 1040-ES titled "How to Pay Estimated Tax." For additional information on filing for a sole proprietor, partners, and/or S corporation shareholder, refer to Publication 505, Tax Withholding and Estimated Tax.

If you are filing as a corporation, you should use Form 1120-W, Estimated Tax for Corporations (PDF), to figure the estimated tax. You must deposit the payment using the Electronic Federal Tax Payment System. For additional information on filing for a corporation, refer to Publication 542, Corporations.

Who Must Pay Estimated Tax

If you are filing as a sole proprietor, partner, S corporation shareholder, and/or a self-employed individual, you generally have to make estimated tax payments if you expect to owe tax of $1,000 or more when you file your return.

If you are filing as a corporation you generally have to make estimated tax payments for your corporation if you expect it to owe tax of $500 or more when you file its return.
If you had a tax liability for the prior year, you may have to pay estimated tax for the current year. See the worksheet in Form 1040-ES (PDF) for more details on who must pay estimated tax.

Who Does Not Have To Pay Estimated Tax

If you receive salaries and wages, you can avoid having to pay estimated tax by asking your employer to withhold more tax from your earnings. To do this, file a new Form W-4 with your employer. There is a special line on Form W-4 for you to enter the additional amount you want your employer to withhold.

You do not have to pay estimated tax for the current year if you **meet all three** of the following conditions.

You had no tax liability for the prior year
You were a U.S. citizen or resident for the whole year
Your prior tax year covered a 12 month period
You had no tax liability for the prior year if your total tax was zero or you did not have to file an income tax return.

For additional information on how to figure your estimated tax, refer to Publication 505, Tax Withholding and Estimated Tax.

Estimated tax requirements are different for farmers and fishermen. Publication 505, Tax Withholding and Estimated Tax, provides more information about these special estimated tax rules.

How To Figure Estimated Tax

To figure your estimated tax, you must figure your expected adjusted gross income, taxable income, taxes, deductions, and credits for the year.

When figuring your estimated tax for the current year, it may be helpful to use your income, deductions, and credits for the prior year as a starting point. Use your prior year's federal tax return as a guide. You can use the worksheet in Form 1040-ES (PDF) to figure your estimated tax. You will need to estimate the amount of income you expect to earn for the year. If you estimated your earnings too high, simply complete another Form 1040-ES worksheet to refigure your estimated tax for the next quarter. If you estimated your earnings too low, again complete another Form 1040-ES worksheet to recalculate your estimated tax for the next quarter. You want to estimate your income as accurately as you can to avoid penalties.

You must make adjustments both for changes in your own situation and for recent changes in the tax law.

When To Pay Estimated Taxes

For estimated tax purposes, the year is divided into four payment periods. Each period has a specific payment due date. If you do not pay enough tax by the due date of each of the payment periods, you may be charged a penalty even if you are due a refund when you file your income tax return. See the Underpayment of Estimated Tax section below for more information.

Using the Electronic Federal Tax Payment System (EFTPS) is the easiest way to pay your federal taxes for individuals as well as businesses. Make **ALL** of your federal tax payments including federal tax deposits (FTDs), installment agreement and estimated tax payments using EFTPS. If it is easier to pay your estimated taxes weekly, bi-weekly, monthly, etc. you can, as long as you have paid enough in by the end of the quarter. Using EFTPS, you can access a history of your payments, so you know how much and when you made your estimated tax payments.

Underpayment of Estimated Tax

If you did not pay enough tax throughout the year, either through withholding or by making estimated tax payments, you may have to pay a penalty for underpayment of estimated tax. Generally, most taxpayers will avoid this penalty if they owe less than $1,000 in tax after subtracting their withholdings and credits, or if they paid at least 90% of the tax for the current year, or 100% of the tax shown on the return for the prior year, whichever is smaller. There are special rules for farmers and fishermen.

However, if your income is received unevenly during the year, you may be able to avoid or lower the penalty by annualizing your income and making unequal payments. Use Form 2210 (PDF), *Underpayment of Estimated Tax by Individuals, Estates, and Trusts*, to see if you owe a penalty for underpaying your estimated tax. Please refer to the Form 1040 Instructions (PDF) or the Form 1040A Instructions for where to report the estimated tax penalty on your return.

The penalty may also be waived if:

The failure to make estimated payments was caused by a casualty, disaster, or other unusual circumstance and it would be inequitable to impose the penalty, or
You retired (after reaching age 62) or became disabled during the tax year for which estimated payments were required to be made or in the preceding tax year, and the underpayment was due to reasonable cause and not willful neglect.

You should also use Form 2210 to request a waiver of the penalty for the reasons shown above.

- *Or to mistakenly think of it as "your money"*

You cannot think in terms of the money you are making as all being yours! You have to calculate at a minimum that only 70% is yours because you will owe something. Most people have no clue or idea on if they owe for a tax year or not and if you are not filing a tax return then it is impossible to even try to calculate what you may owe. I try to keep it simple with clients in my practice and advise them to set aside every month at least 30% to 35% of every dollar so we have it in an account to pay estimated taxes on a monthly basis so they no longer ever find themselves in this situation.

The Collection Process

If you do not pay your tax in full when you file your tax return, you will receive a bill for the amount you owe. This bill starts the collection process, which continues until your account is satisfied or until the IRS may no longer legally collect the tax; for example, when the time or period for collection expires.

The first notice you receive will be a letter that explains the balance due and demands payment in full. It will include the amount of the tax, plus any penalties and interest accrued on your unpaid balance from the date the tax was due.

IRS electronic payment options, available on our Payments page and the IRS2Go app, are the best way for you to pay federal taxes. Paying electronically is a convenient way to make tax payments. You can make electronic payments online, by phone, or from a mobile device. Paying electronically is safe and secure, and the IRS uses the latest encryption technology. You can schedule your payment in advance, and you will receive confirmation after it's submitted. It's quick, easy, secure, and much faster than mailing in a check or money order.

Direct Pay is a secure service you can use to pay your current and prior year 1040 series tax returns and more. Pay directly from your checking or savings account at no cost to you. After you complete five easy steps, you'll receive instant confirmation that your payment has been submitted. With Direct Pay, you can use the "Look Up a Payment" feature to view your payment status. You can modify or cancel your payment there until two business days before your scheduled payment date. However, if you decide to pay by mail, enclose a check or money order with a copy of your notice. Make it payable to the United States Treasury and provide your name, address, daytime phone number, SSN, tax period, and form number (2015 Form 1040) on the front of your payment.

If you cannot pay in full, you should send in as much as you can with the notice and explore other payment arrangements. The unpaid balance is subject to interest that compounds daily and a monthly late payment penalty. It is in your best interest to pay your tax liability in full as soon as you can to minimize the penalty and interest charges. You may want to investigate and consider other methods of financing full payment of your taxes, such as obtaining a cash advance on your credit card or getting a bank loan. Often the rate and any applicable fees your credit card company or bank charges are lower than the combination of interest and penalties imposed by the Internal Revenue Code.

If you are unable to pay your balance in full immediately, the IRS may be able to offer you a monthly installment agreement. To request an installment agreement, you may use the Online Payment Agreement Application (OPA) or complete Form 9465 (PDF), *Installment Agreement Request*, and mail it in with your bill. In some cases, you can establish an installment agreement over the phone.

If you cannot full pay under an installment agreement, you may propose an offer in compromise (OIC). An OIC is an agreement between a taxpayer and the IRS that resolves a taxpayer's tax liability by payment of an agreed upon reduced amount. Before an offer can be considered, all filing and payment requirements must be current. Taxpayers in an open bankruptcy proceeding are not eligible. To confirm eligibility, you may use the Offer in Compromise Pre-Qualifier tool.

If you need more time to pay, you may ask the IRS to delay collection and report your account as currently not collectible. If the IRS determines that you cannot pay any of your tax debt due to a financial hardship, the IRS may temporarily delay collection by reporting your account as currently not collectible until your financial condition improves. Being currently not collectible does not mean the debt goes away. It means the IRS has determined you cannot afford to pay the debt at this time. Prior to approving your request to delay collection, the IRS may ask you to complete a Collection Information Statement and provide proof of your financial status (this may include information about your assets and your monthly income and expenses).

If IRS does delay collecting from you, your debt will continue to accrue penalties and interest until the debt is paid in full. The IRS may temporarily suspend certain collection actions, such as issuing a levy, until your financial condition improves. However, they may still file a Notice of Federal Tax Lien while your account is suspended.

Filing a Notice of Federal Tax Lien
Serving a Notice of Levy, or
Offsetting a refund to which you are entitled

A federal tax lien is a legal claim to your property, including property that you acquire after the lien arises. The federal tax lien arises automatically when you fail to pay in full the taxes you owe within ten days after the IRS makes an assessment of the tax and sends the first notice of taxes owed and demand for payment. The IRS may also file a Notice of Federal Tax Lien in the public records, which publicly notifies your creditors that the IRS has a claim against all your property, including property acquired by you after the filing of the Notice of Federal Tax Lien.

The filing of a Notice of Federal Tax Lien may appear on your credit report and may harm your credit rating. Once a lien arises, the IRS generally cannot release the lien until the tax, penalty, interest, and recording fees are paid in full or until the IRS may no longer legally collect the tax.

The IRS will withdraw a Notice of Federal Tax Lien if the notice was filed while a bankruptcy automatic stay was in effect. The IRS may withdraw a Notice of Federal Tax Lien if the IRS determines:

The Notice was filed too soon or not according to IRS procedures;

You enter into an installment agreement to satisfy the liability unless the installment agreement provides otherwise;

Withdrawal will allow you to pay your taxes more quickly; or
Withdrawal is in your best interest, as determined by the National Taxpayer Advocate, and in the best interest of the government.

The IRS may levy (seize) assets such as wages, bank accounts, social security benefits, and retirement income. The IRS also may seize your property (including your car, boat, or real estate) and sell the property to satisfy the tax debt. In addition, any future federal tax refunds or state income tax refunds that you are due may be seized and applied to your federal tax liability.

- But guess what, if you don't plan and do things properly, 50% of that money belongs to the IRS

As you no doubt can see now that if you ignore filing and paying your taxes 50% or more of what you make is going to go to clean up these horrific problems leaving you with no money. Then your business is interrupted and your life is in a spiral dive downward!

I doubt many people plan to not file or pay their taxes. I think many people are good people who get caught up in life and building a business and dealing with the daily grind.

IRS Notices and Bills, Penalties, and Interest Charges

April 15 is the deadline for most people to file their individual income tax returns and pay any tax owed. During its processing, the IRS checks for mathematical accuracy on your tax return. When processing is complete, if you owe any tax, penalty, or interest, you will receive a bill.

Generally, interest accrues on any unpaid tax from the due date of the return until the date of payment in full. The interest rate is determined quarterly and is the federal short-term rate plus 3 percent. Interest compounds daily.

In addition, if you file a return but don't pay all tax shown as due on time, you will generally have to pay a late payment penalty. The failure to pay penalty is one-half of one percent for each month, or part of a month, up to a maximum of 25% of the amount of tax that remains as unpaid from the due date of the return until paid in full. The one-half of one percent rate increases to one percent if the tax remains unpaid 10 days after the IRS issues a notice of intent to levy property. If you file your return by its due date and request an installment agreement, the one-half of one percent rate decreases to one-quarter of one percent for any month in which an installment agreement is in effect. Be aware that the IRS applies payments to the tax first, then any penalty, then to interest. Any penalty amount that appears on your bill is the total amount of the penalty up to the date of the notice, not the penalty amount charged each month.

If you owe tax and don't file on time, there is a penalty for not filing on time. The failure to file penalty is usually five percent of the tax owed for each month, or part of a month that your return is late, up to a maximum of 25%. If your return is over 60 days late, there is also a minimum penalty for late filing; it is the lesser of $135 or 100 percent of the tax owed unless your failure to file was due to reasonable cause and not willful neglect. You must file your return and pay your tax by the due date to avoid interest and penalty charges. Often, you can borrow the funds necessary to pay your tax at a lower effective rate than the combined IRS interest and penalty rate.

IRS electronic payment options are the best way for you to pay your federal taxes. Electronic payment options are available on IRS.gov/Payments. However, if you decide to pay by mail, in order to make sure your payment credits properly to your account, be sure to return the tear-off stub on your bill and use our return envelope, if provided.

Please ensure that you:

Make your check or money order payable to the United States Treasury
Enter the primary social security number or employer identification number
Enter the tax year and form number
Ensure your name, address, and telephone number are on the payment
Do NOT send cash

The IRS may abate penalties for filing and paying late if you have reasonable cause and the failure was not due to willful neglect. Making a late payment as soon as you are able may help to establish that your initial failure to pay timely was due to reasonable cause and not willful neglect. If billed for penalty charges and you feel you have reasonable cause for abatement, send your explanation along with the bill to your service center, or call the IRS at 800-829-1040 for assistance. Generally, the IRS does not abate interest charges and they continue to accrue until all assessed tax, penalties, and interest are fully paid.

- And that means you're going VERY deeply into debt without realizing it

Enforced Collection Actions

If taxes are not paid timely, and the IRS is not notified why the taxes cannot be paid, the law requires that enforcement action be taken, which could include the following:

Issuing a Notice of Levy on salary and other income, bank accounts or property (legally seize property to satisfy the tax debt)

Assessing a Trust Fund Recovery Penalty for certain unpaid employment taxes
Issuing a Summons to the taxpayer or third parties to secure information to prepare unfiled tax returns or determine the taxpayer's ability to pay

What happens now is that your tax bill begins to grow and grow and grow. It finally becomes so large it would seem impossible to anyone that it could ever be resolved. Meanwhile another new year is at hand and January 1 of the year you begin making money all over and dig the hole even deeper by not paying estimated taxes on the new income in the new tax year.

Pretty soon your boat ha enough water to SINK you and it really gets expensive to now try and figure out how you are going to solve this problem.

- In the past, the IRS moved slowly for various reasons

IRS for any number of reasons in the past may have had less priority on enforcement for non filing returns or not paying your taxes. However the IRS is increasing its automated enforcement efforts using technology enhancements to work 7/24 tracking you down and sending you computer generated notices.

The problem here is once you are in the Automated System everything is on script to happen on certain dates that trigger the next series of enforcement steps as the IRS prepares to use its automated resources to compel you to act. Either file a return, pay your tax or worse yet, pull your account out the automated system and assign it to a Revenue Officer who will likely want to come visit you and have a conversation over a cup of java!!

IRS has upgraded many of its systems and uses an automated system for collections, the ACS Automated Collection System which is an auto pilot collection enforcement tool that can do some real damage real fast!

- It was easy to not file, or file and not pay, and maybe not hear anything for months or years

That was then and this is NOW

IRS is able to do so much more with technology and people make it easy getting on their social media bragging about their bonus checks!!!

With all the local, state and other financial reporting laws virtually everything you do is now reported to the IRS hourly everyday!

When the IRS can make hundreds even thousands of dollars with little in the way of human beings doing the work every hour where do you think the trend is going? Where do you se the future ability of the IRS to track you down like a dog and hammer you!

In my practice we already are seeing results of new technology in the automated enforcement systems. Clients coming in or calling who have not filed for several years all of a sudden opened a bank account or bought a new car or did something that seemed very simple and BANG! IRS got them and now it's time to deal with the devil!

Do NOT be fooled! The IRS will only get better each day and more accurate and capable every week in tracking down virtually everyone who has not filed or paid their taxes. It is only a matter of WHEN!

- I've had clients go YEARS without doing either and getting very little communication from the IRS, until it was too late

One recent case in my practice was a client who had not filed a tax return for eight years! He went to Vegas 2 years ago, got married and guess what; his wife opened a bank account in her name, put him on the account as emergency contact and five weeks later BAM! IRS came knocking on his door. The Agent left a business card so that when he arrived home that afternoon and saw it on the door he freaked out!

Needless to say he was caught!

Now he is in a negotiation with the IRS to file all his returns and work up a proposed payment plan that will include paying over $50,000 in fines! The good news is we actually may be able to help save him from a good part of that financial turmoil but the point is something very simple led to his being located by the IRS and the technology caught up with him.

- The days of the IRS being lax or slow are long gone - it's a different game, you must be ready

The government wants their money and they want it now!

It is a very different game today than even 10 years ago, when for the most part there were not enough resources to chase everyone down and IRS computer systems were still operating in the mid 20th century.

We are in the 21st Century and the IRS is playing catch up really well!

Modernization efforts, upgrading technology and doing more automated enforcement and prosecutions all add to the fact the IRS has a new game book and they are getting really good at finding people and nailing them!

If you have not filed or not paid your taxes, you really want to pay attention to the rest of this ebook and decide how best you will begin to solve your problem.

For the most part many of the problems can be solved by you if you only know what to do and what steps to take and when.

The most important part in solving the problem is first with you deciding you will do it!

Chapter 4
Knowing YOUR Tax Problem

- For the entrepreneur or home-based business owner, you typically fall into one of the following categories:

- You've made money in your business, filed your taxes but haven't fully paid all your taxes
- Or You've made money in your business, filed your taxes but still owe the IRS
- Or You've made money in your business, but haven't filed or paid your taxes
- Why is it important to understand your issue? Because...

Let's take each of these scenarios and look at how you would go about defining what your problem may be and how you would map a solution to it.

- You've made money in your business, filed your taxes but haven't fully paid all your taxes

The first thing you must do is make sure you are staying current on all current year tax obligations and filing of returns. You do not want to take a case where you already owe the IRS and are making payments and make it worse by accumulating more debt to the IRS risking the IRS terminating your installment agreement.

The Easiest Way to Pay All Your Federal Taxes

EFTPS® is a system for paying federal taxes electronically using the Internet, or by phone using the EFTPS® Voice Response System. EFTPS® is offered **free** by the U.S. Department of Treasury.

EFTPS® offers ...
Security, Convenience, Accuracy

Security You Can Count On

EFTPS® is a secure government web site that allows users to make federal tax payments electronically. Every user must have a secure Internet browser with 128-bit encryption in order to access the site. To log on to the system, an enrolled user must be authenticated with three pieces of unique information: Taxpayer Identification Number (EIN or SSN), EFTPS® Personal Identification Number (PIN) and an Internet Password. The combination of these three pieces of identification adds to the security of the site and the privacy of taxpayer data.

Convenience at Your Fingertips

EFTPS® offers you the convenience and flexibility of making your tax payments via the Internet or phone. You can initiate your tax payment from your home or office, 24/7. Businesses and Individuals can schedule payments up to 365 days in advance. Scheduled payments can be changed or cancelled up to two business days in advance of the scheduled payment date.
You can use EFTPS® to make all your federal tax payments, including income, employment, estimated and excise taxes. You can check up to 16 months of your EFTPS® payment history online or by calling EFTPS® Customer Service.

Next you want to make sure you keep current on all your payments with the IRS if you already have an installment agreement. The rules for installment agreements are fairly straight forward;

Understand your agreement & avoid default

Your future refunds will be applied to your tax debt until it is paid in full; Pay at least your minimum monthly payment when it's due; Include your name, address, SSN, daytime phone number, tax year and return type on your payment; File all required tax returns on time & pay all taxes in-full and on time (contact us to change your existing agreement if you cannot); Make all scheduled payments even if we apply your refund to your account balance; and Ensure your statement is sent to the correct address, contact us if you move or complete and mail Form 8822, Change of Address.

If you don't receive your statement, send your payment to the address listed in your agreement.
There may be a reinstatement fee if your agreement goes into default. Penalties and interest continue to accrue until your balance is paid in full. If you are in danger of defaulting on your payment agreement for any reason, contact us immediately. IRS will generally not take enforced collection actions:

When an installment agreement is being considered; While an agreement is in effect; For 30 days after a request is rejected, or During the period the IRS evaluates an appeal of a rejected or terminated agreement.

- Or You've made money in your business, filed your taxes but still owe the IRS

Perhaps you filed your taxes but owe the IRS and have NOT set up an installment agreement plan with the IRS. Again you should set up the EFTPS payment system to stay current on all current year taxes for this year and then work to set up an installment agreement with the IRS on the prior year taxes you owe.

If you're financially unable to pay your tax debt immediately, you can make monthly payments through an installment agreement. As long as you pay your tax debt in full, you can reduce or eliminate your payment of penalties or interest, and avoid the fee associated with setting up the agreement.

Before applying for any payment agreement, you must file all required tax returns. You may be eligible to apply for an online payment agreement;

Individuals must owe $50,000 or less in total combined individual income tax, penalties and interest, and have filed all required returns.

Businesses must owe $25,000 or less in payroll taxes and have filed all required returns.

If you meet these requirements, you can apply for an online payment agreement. Even if you're ineligible for an online payment agreement, you can still pay in installments Complete and mail Form 9465, Installment Agreement Request and Form 433-F, Collection Information Statement; Small Businesses with employees can apply for an in-Business Trust Fund Express installment agreement. These installment agreements generally do not require a financial statement or financial verification as part of the application process.

- Or You've made money in your business, but haven't filed or paid your taxes

In this case it is a little more complicated in that you made money and have not filed a tax return or paid any taxes. The most important thing you can do is FIRST, FILE ALL TAX RETURNS as soon as possible.

File all tax returns that are due, regardless of whether or not you can pay in full. File your past due return the same way and to the same location where you would file an on-time return.

If you have received a notice, make sure to send your past due return to the location indicated on the notice you received.

Why you should file your past due return now

Avoid interest and penalties

File your past due return and pay now to limit interest charges and late payment penalties.

Claim a refund

You risk losing your refund if you don't file your return. If you are due a refund for withholding or estimated taxes, you must file your return to claim it within 3 years of the return due date. The same rule applies to a right to claim tax credits such as the Earned Income Credit. We hold income tax refunds in cases where our records show that one or more income tax returns are past due. We hold them until we get the past due return or receive an acceptable reason for not filing a past due return.

Avoid issues obtaining loans

Loan approvals may be delayed if you don't file your return. Copies of filed tax returns must be submitted to financial institutions, mortgage lenders/brokers, etc., whenever you want to buy or refinance a home, get a loan for a business, or apply for federal aid for higher education.
If you owe more than you can pay

If you cannot pay what you owe, you can request an additional 60-120 days to pay your account in full through the Online Payment Agreement application or by calling 800-829-1040; no user fee will be charged. If you need more time to pay, you can request an installment agreement or you may qualify for an offer in compromise.

What if you don't file voluntarily?

Substitute Return

If you fail to file, we may file a substitute return for you. This return might not give you credit for deductions and exemptions you may be entitled to receive. We will send you a Notice of Deficiency CP3219N (90-day letter) proposing a tax assessment. You will have 90 days to file your past due tax return or file a petition in Tax Court. If you do neither, we will proceed with our proposed assessment. If you have received notice CP3219N you cannot request an extension to file.

If any of the income listed is incorrect, you may do the following:

Contact us at 1-866-681-4271 to let us know.

Contact the payer (source) of the income to request a corrected Form W-2 or 1099.

Attach the corrected forms when you send us your completed tax returns.

If the IRS files a substitute return, it is still in your best interest to file your own tax return to take advantage of any exemptions, credits and deductions you are entitled to receive. The IRS will generally adjust your account to reflect the correct figures.

Collection and enforcement actions

The return we prepare for you (our proposed assessment) will lead to a tax bill, which, if unpaid, will trigger the collection process. This can include such actions as a levy on your wages or bank account or the filing of a notice of federal tax lien.

If you repeatedly do not file, you could be subject to additional enforcement measures, such as additional penalties and/or criminal prosecution.

Help filing your past due return

For filing help, call 1-800-829-1040 or 1-800-829-4059 for TTY/TDD.

If you need wage and income information to help prepare a past due return, complete Form 4506-T, Request for Transcript of Tax Return, and check the box on line 8. You can also contact your employer or payer of income.

If you need information from a prior year tax return, use Get Transcript to request a return or account transcript.

Get our online tax forms and instructions to file your past due return, or order them by calling 1-800-Tax-Form (1-800-829-3676) or 1-800-829-4059 for TTY/TDD.

If you are experiencing a hardship and you can't file your past due return, you can call or write your local Taxpayer Advocate Office for your state.

Once you file your prior year past due returns you now have a second part to your case and that is the payment of the taxes you will owe along with interest and penalties that the IRS will assess and add to the balance. IRS will send you notices of the bill for each tax year you file and then you will need to begin working on the payment process to arrange either to full pay the entire liability of all tax returns you filed late or set up an installment agreement plan.

If you're financially unable to pay your tax debt immediately, you can make monthly payments through an installment agreement. As long as you pay your tax debt in full, you can reduce or eliminate your payment of penalties or interest, and avoid the fee associated with setting up the agreement.

Before applying for any payment agreement, you must file all required tax returns. You may be eligible to apply for an online payment agreement;

Individuals must owe $50,000 or less in total combined individual income tax, penalties and interest, and have filed all required returns.

Businesses must owe $25,000 or less in payroll taxes and have filed all required returns.

If you meet these requirements, you can apply for an online payment agreement.
Even if you're ineligible for an online payment agreement, you can still pay in installments
Complete and mail Form 9465, Installment Agreement Request and Form 433-F, Collection Information Statement;

If you owe the IRS more than $50,000 in total taxes for all the late filed returns you will need to then be prepared to provide the IRS with complete financial disclosure information using IRS Forms 433A and 433B. Setting up an installment agreement for a total liability of more than $50,000 will likely require additional time and effort on your part and you must be careful to use the specific instructions in providing full financial disclosure to the IRS. Here you may wish to consider a consultation so that you are aware of the details and rules involved in setting up an installment agreement with the IRS for a tax debt over $50,000.

Chapter 5
There's a Bloodbath Coming

- As noted, the days of the IRS being slow, and overwhelmed by archaic paper systems are gone

You cannot nor should not assume the IRS is not looking for you simply because you have not received a notice. In fact not having received a notice can actually be a bad thing and could mean your now under a formal investigation depending on the number of tax years you have not filed or the number of tax years you have not paid.

The IRS has identified millions of delinquent returns and has been pursuing a cross-functional National Non-Filer Strategy to identify non-compliant taxpayers and design methods to encourage their compliance. Before contacting a non-filer, the IRS will often attempt to identify the non-filer's occupation, location of bank/savings accounts, sources of income, age, current address, last file return, adjusted gross income of last filed return, taxes paid on last filed return – amounts and methods of payment (withholding, estimated tax, pre-payments), number of years delinquent, and the non-filer's standard of living.

They will search public records for evidence of additional unreported income, tax assessor and real estate records for assets held by the non-filer, and records of professional associations and business license bureaus for information on businesses being operated by the non-filer. They will also search sales tax returns and the state records to disclose corporate charter information including principals of any businesses that have failed to file returns. They will contact the last known employer to determine if the non-filer is still employed and the specific occupation of the non-filer.

If a non-filer is contacted by the IRS, the examiner will determine the cause (does the non-filer lack records, ability to pay, lack of education, etc.) and may offer necessary information or assistance (preparation of returns, payment arrangement information, etc.) to secure full cooperation. If the non-filer is uncooperative (won't respond or refuses to cooperate), third party contacts will be made to determine the non-filer's income.

If the IRS Agent discovers subsequent acts of tax evasion (false statements, refusal to make records available, etc.), they will consider whether the case should be referred for a criminal investigation. The examiner will also be alert to attempts by the non-filer to conceal or transfer assets to evade collection of tax later assessed. In these cases, a jeopardy (immediate) assessment may be considered.

During non-filer examinations, the examiner will determine if related returns (corporate, partnership, employment tax, and excise tax returns) have been filed as required. They will also search for spin-off cases involving relatives, employees, employers, subcontractors, partners, and even return preparers. If a non-filer is involved in a family business, the examiner should determine if all family members have filed returns.

If the non-filer is involved in a partnership, the IRS should determine if partnership returns have been filed and determine if all partners have filed returns. For delinquent corporate returns, they should determine if all shareholders have filed returns. Penalties are not typically be easily waived in non-filer cases without reasonable cause.

If the taxpayer does not respond to government inquiries, the IRS may independently prepare a tax return and the related assessments under Internal Revenue Code § 6020(b). These assessments are generally based on very limited information, such as that gathered from Forms W-2 and 1099.

For these cases, IRS assesses the maximum potential tax owed based on gross receipts since they don't have access to potential deductions, exemptions or credits available to the taxpayer. By failing to file a return, a taxpayer may also lose a refund of any amounts withheld. The failure to file and pay self-employment tax by self-employed individuals could cause them to be ineligible for social security retirement or disability benefits.

- They are now more technically sophisticated than ever, capable of using Google-like algorithms to "crawl" the web for activity that may indicate you are not paying or lying about your taxes

Unfiled Tax Returns

IRS Failure to File Compliance:

Most non-filing investigations of taxpayers initiated by the IRS are based upon computer matches. The IRS uses both a "stop filer program" and a "non-filer program" to discover return delinquencies. If a taxpayer has filed tax returns in the past and then a return is not filed for the next tax period, that taxpayer is identified as a "stop filer". If IRS received information documents (such as Forms W-2 and 1099) which reflect reportable income and no return has been filed then that taxpayer is identified as a "non filer".

Normally the IRS will initiate a non-filing check 15 months after a Form 1040 (Individual Income Tax Return) is due from a "non-filer" or 4 months after the due date for a "stop filer". In the case of business taxes and payroll taxes, such as Form 941 employment tax returns, an IRS delinquency check begins 8 weeks after the due date of a return.

Normally the IRS will attempt to secure returns from "non filers" and "stop filers" by sending Service Center notices requesting that returns be filed. If the taxpayer fails to file despite the computerized notices, the IRS may follow up in several different ways. It may prepare tax returns for the taxpayer based upon information documents it has received from institutions and employers. It may attempt to contact the taxpayer by telephone or it may assign the matter to a Revenue Officer for field investigation.

The Internal Revenue Service delinquency check will normally result in the IRS issuing four (4) computer notices regarding Forms 1040 over a six (6) month period. In the case of business taxes, such as Form 941 for employment taxes, the Internal Revenue Service will normally issue three (3) notices spaced over a period of 22 weeks. IRS collection representatives become involved after the notice phase is completed.

Criminal Non-Filing:

Failing to file returns is a criminal misdemeanor in the federal system. In some instances, failing to file can be prosecuted as a criminal felony. Certain individuals are more likely to be prosecuted by the IRS than others. The complete guidelines regarding criminal non-filing are contained in the Internal Revenue Manual. Here is a partial list of non-filers of interest to the IRS

Criminal Investigation Division:

The non-filing involves known organized crime figures and persons alleged to be receiving graft or income from illegal sources. The taxpayer's occupation and education denote prima facia evidence of knowledge concerning his/her filing obligations. Examples include public officials, attorneys, accountants, stock brokers and business executives.

The non-filer is a tax protester.

In instances where a taxpayer has failed to file returns, he should be alert for indications that the IRS has referred the matter for IRS criminal investigation. If the IRS representative identifies himself as a "special agent", has a gold badge with the words "Criminal Investigation Division" or gives the taxpayer his "rights against self incrimination", that taxpayer should not speak with the IRS representative but should immediately seek legal counsel.

Failure to File Strategies:

For most taxpayers, the act of non-filing is a creditor/debtor issue. The IRS, however, is an extremely aggressive creditor with broad ranging statutory powers to collect tax deficiencies. Unlike regular civil cases and ordinary debt, the IRS need not reduce the tax debt to civil judgment in a court of law; rather the IRS need only rely on the fact that a tax deficiency has been assessed, the taxpayer has been properly noticed of the tax deficiency and noticed of the IRS' intent to levy (a registered letter). The taxpayer must also have failed to pay the tax assessment. Once these prerequisites exist the IRS, as sanctioned through federal statute, may seize and levy upon taxpayer's property. The information in this paragraph presumes the IRS has created a substitute tax return for the non-filer from internal records.

The non-filing client is perhaps the most common IRS collection/controversy problem encountered by tax practitioners. If the tax practitioner is an accountant, the accountant must determine whether the taxpayer has criminal exposure for failure to file returns which is a misdemeanor, or for tax evasion which is a felony. Usually the exposure is there. It is always advisable to refer the client to an attorney in order to protect the client with the attorney-client privilege. An attorney's involvement with a case and initial contact with the IRS can negate IRS interest in a criminal prosecution.

Delinquent returns must be prepared and filed. The question usually arises as to what is the best way to file these returns. There is no single answer to this question although the ultimate goal is always to file the returns. Filing is always a more financially attractive alternative than letting the IRS prepare the returns from internal records. It is possible that an IRS prepared substitute return assessment can be reduced by filing an original return. Additionally, unfiled tax returns do not have a collection statute of limitations. Many clients come to tax practitioners at the last possible moment, usually under aggravated circumstances. Their wages have been garnished or the IRS has levied their bank account. The wage levy in particular has disastrous effects on the employer/employee relationship and the taxpayer's cash flow. A wage garnishment is a "continuing levy" and will not be removed until the taxpayer takes affirmative action in dealing with the IRS. Filing returns is usually a prerequisite to a release of an IRS levy.

Clients are frequently confronted with the following question: "Should I file the return right now, or wait until I have the money to pay for it?". The answer is very simple. The return or returns should be filed as soon as possible. If the client has any funds available for payment, a check should be enclosed with the return. The reason is that non-filing clients are facing one of the highest penalty rates which the IRS is allowed to impose. The failure to file penalty rate is 5% per delinquent month up to a maximum of 25% of the tax due but unpaid by the due date of the return. Filing a timely return without payment, on the other hand, only results in a late payment penalty, which ranges from .05% to 1% per month. In all cases the IRS will add interest at the statutory rates.

- On top of that, they recognize they have billions in outstanding tax payments due; for a country that is trillions in debt, the IRS wants every penny

The IRS Restructuring and Reform Bill of 1998 was a landmark law that put respect for the individual taxpayer back into the system. It forces the IRS to more fully communicate with the public and grant taxpayers "due process" rights.

When the IRS comes around to collect, sooner or later you're going to have to face the music. If you play games with the tax collector, the system is designed to make your life miserable. So here are some things to remember when you owe the IRS:

More people get into more trouble than they've ever bargained for because they ignore those computer-generated IRS notices. Some IRS notices are sent by certified mail. If you think you can ignore these notices by not going to the post office to pick them up, you're mistaken. Respond to the IRS every time.

The IRS has recently revised its publication entitled "The IRS Collection Process." This publication tells you that you have a right to be represented and that you have a right to be treated in a professional and courteous manner. If you do not like the way you are being treated, you can stop the interview and ask to speak with a supervisor.

This may be the best hour you've spent in a long time. The expert will tell you how to prepare for your collection interview, how to conduct yourself and make you aware of when the IRS revenue officer is attempting to take advantage of you. You must always remember that the IRS revenue officer's job is to collect money for the Government.

IRS collection interviews are no picnic and you should have representation. Chances are you will wind up with much better results with representation accompanying you. The IRS was recently "audited" by the General Accounting Office and it seems the IRS' own house needs some cleaning. Often, the IRS cannot keep track of how much you owe, especially if you have been making regular payments. The IRS makes mistakes, don't take their word for things.

The IRS can no longer simply take your bank account, your automobile, your business or garnish your wages without giving you written notice and an opportunity to challenge what the IRS claims. When you challenge the IRS, all collection activity must come to a screeching halt. You can even take the IRS to court and they cannot collect from you until the judge issues a decision. You can literally tie the IRS' hands for years. The IRS is not going to tell you what to do or how to protect yourself.

Are you widowed, divorced or separated? Do you have tax problems that arose out of the actions of your former spouse? If you answered yes to any of these questions, you may be entitled to innocent spouse relief. This relief could result in the entire tax bill being written off against you. Yes, individual states also grant innocent spouse relief. In this country, no one goes to jail for owing taxes. You can go to jail for cheating on your taxes and you can go to jail for trying to trick the tax collector, you can go to jail for not filing your taxes, but you can't go to jail simply because you owe the IRS and can't pay.

People who owe taxes, whether to the IRS or their home state, generally have several options available to them. First, if you owe and can pay in full, you should pay the taxes despite the pain. However, if you cannot pay in full, four avenues may be open to you:

Hardship suspension. Here the IRS leaves you alone temporarily. Your account will be reviewed periodically for your ability to pay. Even though the IRS will not bother you, interest continues to accrue on your account and is compounded daily.

Installment payment arrangement. Here the IRS allows you to make monthly installment payments. Ideally, the IRS wants the bill paid in full within three years. You complete a financial statement and essentially pursue a conventional bank loan. Interest continues to accrue and is compounded daily on the remaining balance.

Bankruptcy. It's not for everyone. However, some taxes, usually income taxes, state and federal, may be dischargeable in a Chapter 7 bankruptcy proceeding. Other bankruptcy chapters allow you to pay your tax bill in monthly installments with either little or no interest at all. Bankruptcy rules are complicated. See a qualified bankruptcy attorney who understands both bankruptcy law and tax law.

Offer in compromise. This is the IRS version of "let's make a deal". Under certain circumstances, the IRS will accept the payment of a smaller sum as payment in full for a larger tax debt. Individual states have similar procedures. If your offer is accepted, tax liens are removed and you are given a fresh start. You should consult with an attorney who specializes in these offers.

IRS tax collectors have more power than just about anyone in the federal government. They operate under very few rules. They can make your life pleasant or miserable. Most success in dealing with tax collectors comes from your communicating with them in a prompt manner. Here is a sampling of what they can do:

- File a tax lien against you;
- Levy your bank account;
- Garnish your wages;
- Close down your business;
- Seize and sell your home;
- Damage employment and business relationships;
- Assess you personally for corporate employment taxes;
- Put you in a monthly installment payment arrangement that is too high;
- Contact your banker, neighbors, friends and business relationships concerning your tax liabilities;
- Go after third party transferees of your assets.

- So they've staffed up more than at any time in history, with dedicated teams to go after people in your position (who make well above average income and yet don't pay)...this includes teams that watch social media (don't post about your Ferrari on Facebook, okay?)

Meanwhile, the scope and complexity of the global financial system — and thus the need for robust IRS enforcement — continue to expand. Estimates suggest that the international tax gap (that is, the amount of unpaid U.S. taxes each year on cross-border transactions) is between $40 billion and $133 billion.

Weakening IRS enforcement ultimately hurts the entire budget and increases deficits. A dollar spent on enforcement yields a significant return by increasing the collection of revenue that is due under current law. The Treasury estimates that, from current levels, every additional dollar invested in IRS tax enforcement activities yields $6 in increased revenue. Further, increased enforcement funding produces indirect revenue savings by deterring tax evasion, which Treasury estimates to be at least three times the direct revenue impact.

As Commissioner Koskinen summarized, "Essentially, the government is losing billions to achieve budget savings of a few hundred million dollars."

IRS has two essential IT projects: Information Reporting and Documentation Matching, designed to match documents such as 1099-K forms with individual tax returns to help track down underreported income; and the Return Review Program, designed to replace the outmoded Electronic Fraud Detection System, the IRS's main system for detecting fraudulent returns. Part of an aggressive IRS effort to prevent identity thieves from obtaining tax refunds fraudulently, the Return Review Program is meant to keep the IRS "ahead of identity thieves because we will be able to act more quickly to incorporate what we learn about fraud schemes into our filters," Koskinen says.

IRS Responsibilities Growing

Another major new set of responsibilities for the IRS concerns the Foreign Account Tax Compliance Act (FATCA). Enacted in 2010, FATCA seeks to reduce illegal tax evasion by requiring filers and financial institutions to report more information to the IRS about assets held in offshore accounts. More than 150,000 financial institutions in 112 countries have already registered under FATCA. The IRS needs added personnel and IT resources to collect and analyze the large amounts of information that FATCA will generate and to conduct enforcement activities where warranted.

Finally, the number of individual income tax returns grew by nearly 7 million, or 5 percent, between 2010 and 2014, and will likely continue to grow. The increasing number of tax returns means that more people will continue to not file or pay their taxes each year.

- This is going to lead to an unprecedented number of summons, arrests and jailing of people--more than any time in history

Investigative Process

Part 9. Chapter 5 of the Internal Revenue Manual comprises the bulk of the material used in court and taught to IRS-CI Agents during their six month sojourn at the Federal Law Enforcement Training Centers (FLETC) in Glynco, GA. IRS-CI Agents in training focus heavily on three primary "Methods of Proof" to help produce conviction in the minds of a judge or jury. These methods include: 1) Specific Items, 2) Net Worth, 3) Expenditures, and relate primarily to evidence gathering based on how an individual has acquired their wealth - *"Part 9. Criminal Investigation, Chapter 5. Investigative Process, Section 9. Methods of Proof". irs.gov. March 19, 2012.* Each method seeks to compare a suspects standard of living and sources of income to that income reported for tax purposes.

Direct - Specific Item Method

Under this method the government seeks to substantiate specific items that were not reported completely or accurately for tax purposes. The government must also show that the items of omission were made willfully to understate the subjects tax liability.

There are three broad categories of schemes which are suited to the specific item method of proof:

Understatement of income
Overstatement of expenses
Fraudulent claims for credits or exemptions

Indirect – Net-Worth Method

The IRS considers the net worth method a very effective way of proving taxable income in criminal tax investigations, and states.

The formula for calculating the subject's correct taxable income can be broken down into four steps:
The special agent must first calculate the change in a subject's net worth (assets less liabilities). This is done by determining the subject's net worth at the beginning and end of a period of time (a taxable year or years) and then subtracting the beginning period's net worth figure from the ending period's net worth figure. This computation will yield a change in net worth (either an increase or decrease in net worth).

The amount of this change in net worth is then adjusted for personal living expenses, nondeductible losses, and nontaxable items to arrive at a corrected adjusted gross income figure.
The corrected adjusted gross income figure is then adjusted for itemized deductions or the standard deduction amount, and then for exemptions, to arrive at a corrected taxable income figure.

Finally, by comparing the corrected taxable income figure with the taxable income reported on the tax return, the special agent can determine whether the subject failed to report any taxable income.

Indirect - Expenditures Method

"It starts with an appraisal of the subject's net worth situation at the beginning of a period. He may have much or he may have nothing. If during that period, his expenditures have exceeded the amount he returned as income and his net worth at the end of the period is the same as it was at the beginning (or any difference accounted for), then it may be concluded that his income tax return shows less income than he has in fact received. Of course it is necessary, so far as possible to negate nontaxable receipts by the subject during the period in question."

Sources of Evidence

Agents rely heavily on 3rd party testimony and many tips originate from an inside source, such as a perturbed business partner or ex-wife. Other valuable sources of information include tax returns, trash (legally acquired from outside of the home's curtilage), purchases, SARs - Suspicious activity report, subpoenaed cell phones records, computer files, insider testimony, telephone tapping, subpoena's, etc.

- 3 examples of everyday people getting slapped

Husband and Wife Sentenced on Tax Charges

On Sept. 16, 2014, in Denver, Colorado, Mathew Zuckerman, of Woody Creek, Colorado, was sentenced to 24 months in prison, three years of supervised release and ordered to pay $693,706 in restitution to the IRS. Zuckerman's wife, Sandra Zuckerman was sentenced to 36 months' probation and was jointly liable for $112,511 of the restitution. Mathew Zuckerman pleaded guilty on Feb. 18, 2014, to income tax evasion and Sandra Zuckerman pleaded guilty on May 30, 2014, to willful failure to pay income taxes. According to court documents, beginning in 1986 and continuing through 2009, the Zuckermans either failed to file an income tax return, or filed a return using incorrect income amounts. Matthew Zuckerman concealed his assets and business affairs from the IRS by utilizing corporations and trusts in order to avoid payment and collection of the Zuckerman's outstanding tax liabilities. In 1999, the Zuckermans caused the deed to their Woody Creek residence, purchased for approximately $1.2 million, to be recorded in the name of a Nevada corporation that listed the names of a cat and a dog as its officers and directors. Similarly, in 2004 Mathew Zuckerman formed a company in Nevada that was used to purchase a $1.8 million home in 2004. Furthermore, in December 2004, Mathew Zuckerman formed and used a trust to receive profits in excess of $500,000 while evading payments of taxes owed to the IRS.

Mississippi Businessman Sentenced for Failing to File Taxes

On Sept. 9, 2014, in New Orleans, Mississippi, Kendall O. Marquar, of Waveland, was sentenced to 12 months of home detention after pleading guilty to willfully failing to file taxes. In addition, Marquar was ordered to pay $156,941 in restitution to the IRS and a $3,162 fine. According to court documents, from in or around 2000 through in or around 2012, Marquar, a Mississippi businessman, owned a company called K&D Earthworks that was a maintenance and construction vendor at the Orleans Parish Sheriff's Office (OPSO). During the years 2007, 2008, and 2009, Marquar and K&D Earthworks earned approximately $580,379 in taxable income, mainly from work performed at the OPSO. Marquar failed to file taxes during the years 2007 through 2009.

Texas Man Sentenced For Tax Evasion

On Aug. 21, 2014, in San Antonio, Texas, Daniel Isiah Thody was sentenced to 90 months in prison, three years of supervised release and ordered to pay $162,857 restitution to the Internal Revenue Service. On Nov. 8, 2013, a jury convicted Thody on five counts of tax evasion. According to court documents, Thody willfully evaded and failed to file income tax returns for calendar years 2006 through 2010. Thody intentionally tried to conceal from the IRS his true income by using another individual's bank account as well as the name of a nominee company--WET Publishing—a company created by his father to produce anti-government publications.

- You are a target, and they won't give you warning

The IRS estimates that approximately 10 to 12 million taxpayers fail to file their federal income tax returns each year which results in large amounts of back taxes and fees. The reasons are varied: some taxpayers simply procrastinate; others don't understand their filing requirement; and in a few cases, taxpayers willfully fail to file in an attempt to evade their responsibility to report their income and pay their tax liability. Regardless of the reason, the IRS identifies all of these taxpayers as "non-filers." In most instances, the problems faced by non-filers can be resolved successfully if the taxpayer obtains experienced professional advice and voluntarily addresses the problem. On the other hand, the continuing failure of a taxpayer to voluntarily comply with tax return filing and to obtain experienced counsel can result in severe consequences. In some cases, a taxpayer may even suffer criminal tax prosecution for failure to file returns.

Delinquent returns are often more closely examined by the IRS. For that reason, along with others, the preparation and filing of a delinquent tax return requires an extra level of care and accuracy. When filing delinquent tax returns, it is important to move quickly and correctly, and to follow IRS guidelines for "voluntary compliance." If handled properly, the problem can often be resolved successfully; if handled in the wrong way, the chance of criminal prosecution or other enforced collection activity increases.

Identifying Non-Filers

For many years, the IRS lacked the budget and the ability to identify and find habitual non-filers. However, the IRS has substantially increased its budget for technology that will enable it to find and pursue taxpayers who fail to regularly file their returns. The IRS has targeted the problem of non-filers as one of its highest priorities. The IRS has developed and continues to improve sophisticated computer matching and software programs designed to identify and locate these taxpayers. IRS computer capabilities are constantly being improved to enable the agency to match third-party income and expense information returns with taxpayers. If you have not filed all required tax returns, and have not yet been discovered by the IRS, the time to act is now. If you fail to act now, the IRS is almost certain to knock on your door in the future. Willful failure to file a tax return is a misdemeanor carrying a maximum sentence of one year in prison for each tax year. Worse yet, tax evasion is a felony carrying a maximum sentence of five years in prison for each tax year. Do not risk criminal tax prosecution. Obtain voluntary compliance with your income tax return filing obligations now.

IRS Non-Filer Program

Between the late 1990s and 2004, the IRS conducted an intensive research program of non-filers. This study resulted in an IRS determination that approximately 10 to 12 million taxpayers annually fail to file their income tax returns. In response, the IRS created a joint task force of revenue agents and tax auditors from the IRS Examination Division, revenue officers from the Collection Division, and special agents from the Criminal Investigation Division to locate non-filers and secure compliance with filing requirements. Although the task force secured a number of delinquent tax returns, it did not substantially reduce the number of taxpayers who regularly fail to file their tax return. The IRS continues to flag the non-filer problem as a high priority and continues to develop its ability to locate these taxpayers.

The IRS Information Reporting System (IRP) is a multi-task system and contains a subsystem aimed at the discovery of under-reporting of income and taxpayers who have not filed their required tax returns. This subsystem is the backbone of the IRS effort to identify and locate non-filers. The non-filer subsystem program matches information documents such as W-2s and 1099s to the information reported by the taxpayer and is most responsible to discovering most non-filers. Depending on the filing requirements, information documents are submitted by the payers and receivers to governmental agencies. In addition, this subsystem is used in the IRS stop-filer program to identify taxpayers who have filed returns in the past, but have failed to file returns for the current tax year.

Voluntary Compliance

In many cases, if a taxpayer seeks to correct the problem before an IRS investigation or examination, it is possible to use the IRS's "voluntary disclosure" policy to file missing returns and avoid prosecution. In connection with the voluntary compliance program, the taxpayer must be careful to file returns that are accurate and truthful. If the IRS determines that late-filed returns are false, the chances of criminal prosecution increase tremendously. The IRS's voluntary disclosure policy applies to a taxpayer who:

- Voluntarily informs the IRS of his failure to file for one or more years
- Had income from only legal sources

- Makes the disclosure prior to being informed that he is under criminal investigation
- Files a correct tax return or cooperates with the IRS in ascertaining his correct tax liability
- Makes full payment of the amount due, or if unable to do so, makes bona fide arrangements to pay

Enforced Compliance

Once the IRS identifies and locates a non-filer or stop-filer, the agency begins to send a series of notices requesting that delinquent returns be filed. Usually, the IRS will send a series of four computer-generated notices (often referred to as CP Notices) to the taxpayer prior to initiating personal visits or telephone contact. Individual taxpayers receive these CP Notices over a 26-week period, while business taxpayers normally receive at least three notices during a 22-week period. If the taxpayer fails or refuses to respond to the computerized notices, the IRS uses a variety of methods to force compliance. The IRS may prepare its own tax return for the taxpayer based on third-party documents and information returns filed with the agency. It may also attempt to contact the taxpayer by telephone or assign the case to a Revenue Officer for field investigation.

If telephone contact is warranted, the case will be assigned to the Automated Collection System (ACS). Once contacted by ACS personnel, the taxpayer will be asked to file his or her delinquent returns. ACS employees may also contact neighbors, employers and others in an attempt to secure information about the taxpayer's potential tax liability. Once the IRS secures adequate information about a non-filer's income and the taxpayer fails to voluntarily file a return, the IRS will often prepare its own Substitute for Return (SFR) on behalf of the taxpayer.

Substitute for Returns

Substitute For Returns (SFRs) are prepared and filed pursuant to authority granted the Internal Revenue Service by IRC §6020(b) which authorizes the IRS to prepare an individual income tax return on behalf of the taxpayer. In most cases, the Automated Substitute for Return (ASFR) system is used to evaluate the IRS Master File (MF) information about the taxpayer, and prepare an SFR for a wage earner or taxpayer without other unresolved taxpayer delinquent accounts (TDAs). In order to conserve manpower and financial resources, cases having the following criteria will generally be handled by the ASFR system: (1) The taxpayer is not self-employed; (2) total income is less than $100,000; (3) the income shown on the IRS Information Reporting System totals more than 75% of adjusted gross income and total positive income on the taxpayer's last filed return; (4) the tax year is no older than six years prior to the current tax year; (5) there is no current or pending "uncollectible status" on the account; and (6) the taxpayer's address has been verified. If these conditions do not exist, the matter will be sent to a Revenue Officer to review and obtain pertinent information prior to referral to the Examination Division for creation of an SFR for the taxpayer.

Criminal Non-Filing

If the IRS discovers a habitual non-filer before voluntary disclosure, either through its own non-filer programs or through an informant, the IRS will often refer the matter to the Criminal Investigation Division (CID) to determine if criminal prosecution is warranted. The IRS has devoted substantial resources to identifying non-filers. Most often, the IRS Criminal Investigation Division targets "high-impact" individuals, taxpayers that habitually file "non-processable returns" and "Tax Protestors" for criminal prosecution. IRS special agents assigned to the CID also evaluate the information obtained in their investigation to identify certain activities, called "badges of fraud," that may indicate criminal tax fraud.

Chapter 6
Games the IRS Plays

- Here's what the IRS can do to you if you're 1,2, 5 years or more unfiled returns or unpaid taxes

Regardless of what some commentators may tell you, it is not only lawful, but also Constitutional to pay taxes. With the exception of people who make less than the federal exemption amount, everyone must file a tax return with the federal government. Intentionally failing to file a tax return can result in stiff penalties including up to one year in prison and $100,000 in fines along with the prosecution costs for each year you do not file.

Over the past three years, more than half of the cases that the IRS investigated for failure to file taxes resulted in prosecution. Out of those prosecuted, 78 percent were indicted and served an average of 40 months in prison along with paying all withheld taxes, interest, and prosecution fees. There are some common ways in which an investigation is commenced.

Whistle Blowers

The first and most common trigger the IRS uses for locating people who are not filing a tax return in the whistle blower program. The whistle blower program offers people who report non-filers a percentage of the collected taxes and fees once the prosecution is complete. However, the reward is only guaranteed if the amount is over $2 million. Common whistle blowers include business accountants and employees. Ex-spouses, ex-partners, former employees, neighbors, virtually everyone you know could be a potential whistle blower out for the reward.

Random Audit

An IRS investigation into non-filing begins with random audit programs. The IRS will typically find a tax form such as a W-2 from an employer or business that does not have any matching income reporting. The person listed is researched and their identity found. Once the person is located, the IRS makes every attempt to contact the individual and assist them with their tax filings.

Some other things that have shown up in IRS random audits leading to prosecution included fraudulent EIN codes, businesses who accept funds under the table and are unregistered with the IRS, and couples who are running an unregistered business using their home.

Associations

One area that the IRS now specifically targets on a regular basis are political or financial organizations that claim they have ways of helping people avoid filing. Labeled by the IRS as frivolous tax arguments, the propagators of these arguments are hunted down and prosecuted on a regular basis. There are numerous people who are members of these associations whom the IRS considers suspicious and immediately investigates for tax related crimes such as not filing a tax return.

Solution

The penalties for refusal to file taxes are harsh. If the IRS prevails, you will lose your freedom, your career, and will be held accountable for repaying extensive IRS fees and back-owed taxes. On top of everything else, your case will be published on the IRS website for the world to see. If the IRS confronts you about filing your taxes, comply and end the matter in its entirety as quickly as possible.

Willie Nelson and Wesley Snipes

Look At Willie Nelson and Wesley Snipes. Both had high profile cases with the IRS and both suffered serious consequences.

Willie Nelson did not pay over $6.5 million in income taxes; he ended up with penalties totaling over $10 million. Since he could not come up with the money to pay, the IRS seized most of his property and sold it for his back taxes.

Wesley Snipes tax problems took place in 2008. In April of that year, he was sentenced to three years in prison for failure to file income tax returns. He was sentenced to misdemeanors but only narrowly escaped more serious felony charges because he was able to convince the court that he got caught up in believing the wrong advisors who said that income taxes were illegal.

Enforcement Tools

The IRS has numerous enforcement tools and can deploy these to compel payment of taxes. What is important to note is while you have rights under the Taxpayer Bill of Rights, if you ignore the notices you miss deadlines and waive important appeal rights.

- Liens against property

When the federal government calculates that you have a tax liability, they bill you (by sending you what is called, in IRS-speak, a "notice of demand"). You will then have ten days to pay the debt in full. If you do nothing, one action the government might take is to file a Notice of Federal Tax Lien. If you still do nothing, consider this: once they have filed a lien, the IRS is a short step away from seizing your bank accounts and garnishing your wages. This is serious stuff. The Notice publicly lets your creditors know that the federal government has a claim against your property. The lien is a claim against all your property (your house, your car, etc.). It is a claim against your rights to property (your accounts receivable, for example, if you are an employer), or potentially any other property you acquire in the future.

You may challenge the original tax liability—and thus the lien itself—if you feel it is not accurate. When a Notice is first filed against you for a given tax period, you have thirty days to request a hearing with the IRS's Office of Appeals. The appeals process offers two main procedures. The most relevant one for this discussion, the Collection Due Process (CDP), is available to certain taxpayers, including those with a lien against their property. CDP allows you to go to court if you do not agree with the appeals decision. For more on IRS collection appeals, see IRS publication 1660.

When a lien is filed against you, your credit rating may take a devastating hit, potentially making it nearly impossible for you to qualify for a loan, get a credit card, or sign a lease. If a lien is filed against you and you do not plan to appeal it, your first priority should be to get that Notice of Federal Tax Lien "released."

Release of the Notice of Federal Tax Lien is issued within thirty days after you fully pay the debt—including interest and any penalties—or by having the debt adjusted. The lien is also released within that same time frame if you submit a bond that guarantees payment of the debt, including all of the fees charged by the state or other jurisdictions to file and release the lien.
Though the lien is on your property, you still might be able to use that property as collateral for further financing in order to meet your tax obligation. In other words, the IRS might be willing to put its claim to your assets after those of a private financer willing to give you a home equity loan. Read about it in IRS publication 784 for details.

Usually, a lien is released automatically after ten years, provided Uncle Sam has not re-filed the Notice. If a Notice of Federal Tax Lien should be released and is not—whether deliberately or negligently—you have the right to sue the federal government (but not any IRS employees) for damages.

The full amount of your lien is a matter of public record. It remains so until it is paid in full. However, at any time, you can request that your lien payoff amount be updated to reflect the remaining balance due. Just call the IRS's toll-free customer service telephone number, 1-800-913-6050. You can arrange to receive a letter with the current amount you must pay before the Notice of Federal Tax Lien is released.

- IRS Seizures, Liens, Levies, and other enforcement

IRS tax collection procedures

According to IRS tax collection procedures, the IRS can do a number of things in order to collect what you owe, such as:

Attaching wages.
One IRS tax collection procedure allows the IRS to levy between 30-70 percent of a taxpayer's wages to pay for a tax debt. The IRS can levy Social Security income; however they are limited in the amount they can levy.

Putting liens on property.
Another IRS tax collection tactic is to place a lien on any property that you own, such as your home, business and even your car. A property lien stays in effect until the IRS tax debt is paid in full or the debt expires.

Attaching levies.
IRS tax collection may also include attaching levies to your bank account. A bank levy freezes your account, prohibiting you from accessing any of the funds, and the IRS can withdraw all of the money in your account as payment on your IRS tax debt.

Seizing assets.
Finally, IRS tax collection may include seizing assets. While this is incredibly rare, the IRS will use this method in large tax avoidance schemes. The IRS often uses property seizures to make a public statement that if somebody tries to abuse the tax system, they will seize their property.

The IRS cannot freeze and seize monies in your bank account without proper notice. This is another tactic by the IRS to get your attention. Once your bank receives a notice of seizure of your funds, your bank has an obligation to hold the money for at least 15 days before paying it over to the IRS. You must contact the IRS immediately to negotiate either a partial or a full release of your funds.

Seizing bank assets.

When is the IRS Required to Release My Bank Account?

Under federal law, the IRS must release your bank account if:

You pay the tax, penalty, and interest you owe.

You discover the time for collection (the statute of limitations) ended before the levy was served.

You provide documentation proving that releasing the levy will help them collect the tax.

You have an installment agreement, or enter into one, unless the agreement says the levy does not have to be released.

You determine that the levy is creating a significant economic hardship for you.

The fair market value of the property exceeds such liability and release of the levy on a part of such property could be made without hindering the collection of such liability.

The IRS may consider releasing your funds when:

They levy before they send you the two required notices, or before your time for responding to them has passed (10 days for the Notice and Demand, 30 days for the Notice of Intent to Levy, and the Notice of Right to a Hearing). They did not follow their own procedures. They agree to let you pay in installments, but they still levy, and the agreement does not say that they can do so. Returning the property will help you pay your taxes. Returning the property is in your best interest and the government's best interest.

IRS tax collection limits:

Are there any?

Although it's clear that IRS tax collection abilities are far-reaching, rest assured that disputing tax debts is an option and that the IRS does have limits when it comes to tax collection . They must give every taxpayer multiple chances to resolve their IRS tax debt before they enforce collection action. Also, before attaching a levy to a taxpayer's bank account or wages, the IRS must send a final notice, giving the taxpayer 30 days to dispute the collection action being proposed or to make the full payment.

- Note: in every scenario, the IRS will try to maximize the legal and financial penalty, making you as in debt and beholden to them as possible

It is critical to understand that if you have not filed a tax return for two or more years you really should make a decision to resolve these issues sooner vs later. You truly are playing with fire and taking a chance on significant fines say nothing for your freedom when you go to federal prison!

The fines, interest and penalties stack up on top of the taxes, then you begin to live your life in constant reaction mode always on the DEFENSE and waiting for the next shoe to drop. The IRS will use every tool it has in its arsenal to compel you to meet your filing, reporting and payment obligations. The more we embrace technology the more the IRS will use that technology to snag you and reel you into the world of enforcement!

- You MUST assume the worst, until you are 100% prepared

Whatever you decide to do you should assume the worst possible thing could happen and you could come home tomorrow to meet an IRS Notice or worse yet, an IRS Agent waiting for you outside your home!

You should be 100% prepared to begin dealing with the problems You should obtain a full transcript of your IRS computer account files to see where you are at.

You should begin organizing each tax year by year and begin gathering all records.

You should set a deadline that you will work toward to file all unfiled returns

Then-

You should get started on solving your problem

It will only get worse and the bill will only get higher the longer you put it off. You risk civil penalties, fines and even jail time by ignoring the problem and the IRS is getting really good now at tracking you down with social media tools.

Chapter 7
Knowing Your Real Rights

- You don't have to deal directly with the IRS, someone can do it for you

Under the Taxpayer Bill of Rights you have absolute rights under the law and one of those rights important to solving your problem is the right to be represented before the IRS by an attorney, CPA or an Enrolled Agent.

<u>Summary of Taxpayer Bill of Rights</u>

Taxpayer Bill of Rights
Each and every taxpayer has a set of fundamental rights they should be aware of when dealing with the IRS. Explore your rights and our obligations to protect them.

The Right to Be Informed
The Right to Quality Service
The Right to Pay No More than the Correct Amount of Tax
The Right to Challenge the IRS's Position and Be Heard
The Right to Appeal an IRS Decision in an Independent Forum
The Right to Finality
The Right to Privacy
The Right to Confidentiality
The Right to Retain Representation
The Right to a Fair and Just Tax System

Let's examine each of these important rights you have under the law.

<u>The Right to Be Informed</u>

Taxpayers have the right to know what they need to do to comply with the tax laws. They are entitled to clear explanations of the laws and IRS procedures in all tax forms, instructions, publications, notices, and correspondence. They have the right to be informed of IRS decisions about their tax accounts and to receive clear explanations of the outcomes.

The Right to Quality Service
Taxpayers have the right to receive prompt, courteous, and professional assistance in their dealings with the IRS, to be spoken to in a way they can easily understand, to receive clear and easily understandable communications from the IRS, and to speak to a supervisor about inadequate service.

The Right to Pay No More than the Correct Amount of Tax
Taxpayers have the right to pay only the amount of tax legally due, including interest and penalties, and to have the IRS apply all tax payments properly.

The Right to Challenge the IRS's Position and Be Heard
Taxpayers have the right to raise objections and provide additional documentation in response to formal IRS actions or proposed actions, to expect that the IRS will consider their timely objections and documentation promptly and fairly, and to receive a response if the IRS does not agree with their position.

The Right to Appeal an IRS Decision in an Independent Forum
Taxpayers are entitled to a fair and impartial administrative appeal of most IRS decisions, including many penalties, and have the right to receive a written response regarding the Office of Appeals' decision. Taxpayers generally have the right to take their cases to court.

The Right to Finality
Taxpayers have the right to know the maximum amount of time they have to challenge the IRS's position as well as the maximum amount of time the IRS has to audit a particular tax year or collect a tax debt. Taxpayers have the right to know when the IRS has finished an audit.

The Right to Privacy

Taxpayers have the right to expect that any IRS inquiry, examination, or enforcement action will comply with the law and be no more intrusive than necessary, and will respect all due process rights, including search and seizure protections and will provide, where applicable, a collection due process hearing.

The Right to Confidentiality

Taxpayers have the right to expect that any information they provide to the IRS will not be disclosed unless authorized by the taxpayer or by law. Taxpayers have the right to expect appropriate action will be taken against employees, return preparers, and others who wrongfully use or disclose taxpayer return information.

The Right to Retain Representation

Taxpayers have the right to retain an authorized representative of their choice to represent them in their dealings with the IRS. Taxpayers have the right to seek assistance from a Low Income Taxpayer Clinic if they cannot afford representation.

The Right to a Fair and Just Tax System

Taxpayers have the right to expect the tax system to consider facts and circumstances that might affect their underlying liabilities, ability to pay, or ability to provide information timely. Taxpayers have the right to receive assistance from the Taxpayer Advocate Service if they are experiencing financial difficulty or if the IRS has not resolved their tax issues properly and timely through its normal channels.

- They don't have to seize money or lien - if you do this

If you have not filed or have not paid your taxes you are ALWAYS better to start sooner vs later. You have significant advantages in negotiating a settlement and controlling the outcome from an offensive posture vs defense. When you are on defense you have to react to all the variables many of which you will not know or expect.

Use your appeal rights, make sure you know exactly where you are at in the process as to defining your problem so you can be successful in mapping out a solution.

- You can defer enforcement while your taxes are being figured out

Many Americans owe taxes to the Internal Revenue Service (IRS), but simply don't have the money to pay them. While it's tempting to avoid filing your tax returns to delay the IRS knowing that you have a balance due, that is actually the more costly and problematic method of dealing with the problem. This will only result in more that you will eventually have to pay after adding interest and penalties. The penalties can escalate up to as much as 75% of the tax in some cases and then you find the total very hard to pay.

Even filing for an extension is not a solution when you do not have the money to pay your tax debt. Filing for an extension is an extension to file; it is not an extension to pay. Filing your returns on time ensures that you avoid the failure to file penalty, and helps you get your tax debt resolved in a smoother and timelier fashion, also reducing your interest and late payment penalties.

One important thing to note is that if you ignore letters and notices from the IRS regarding paying your tax, they will eventually garnish your wages, levy your bank accounts, puts liens on your assets, and put negative information on your credit report. IRS wage garnishment is a serious issue because they are allowed to garnish most of your wages. The amount of wages that are exempt from garnishment is the amount of the personal exemption credit. There are other rules that involve support and court ordered payments, but the point is that you risk serious financial chaos when you ignore the problem.

You should realize, however, that there are rules regarding the installment plans. You must honor the monthly due dates, or you risk having your plan cancelled. You also have to make certain that for future years, you have sufficient withholding or estimated payments, to ensure that you will not have a balance due in the future. The IRS will be somewhat lenient if you have a balance due that you cannot pay promptly two years in a row, but will be less than cooperative if it goes on for a third year.

- You don't have to pay your full bill - and you never should

The Right to Pay No More than the Correct Amount of Tax

Taxpayers have the right to pay only the amount of tax legally due, including interest and penalties, and to have the IRS apply all tax payments properly.

If the IRS filed an SFR return for you, then you can challenge that the tax may be wrong or incorrect. You will want to make voluntary payments on the amount that you believe is what you owe while you work to appeal or challenge the amounts you do not believe you owe. Penalties will not go away since you have not filed returns on time but it is likely you could end up with a much lower liability once you file the returns.

- You can make minimum payments that work for you

People who owe taxes, whether to the IRS or their home state, generally have several options available to them. First, if you owe and can pay in full, you should pay the taxes despite the pain. However, if you cannot pay in full, four avenues may be open to you:

Hardship suspension. Here the IRS leaves you alone temporarily. Your account will be reviewed periodically for your ability to pay. Even though the IRS will not bother you, interest continues to accrue on your account and is compounded daily.

Installment payment arrangement. Here the IRS allows you to make monthly installment payments. Ideally, the IRS wants the bill paid in full within three years. You complete a financial statement and essentially pursue a conventional bank loan. Interest continues to accrue and is compounded daily on the remaining balance.

Bankruptcy. It's not for everyone. However, some taxes, usually income taxes, state and federal, may be dischargeable in a Chapter 7 bankruptcy proceeding. Other bankruptcy chapters allow you to pay your tax bill in monthly installments with either little or no interest at all. Bankruptcy rules are complicated. See a qualified bankruptcy attorney who understands both bankruptcy law and tax law.

Offer in compromise. This is the IRS version of "let's make a deal". Under certain circumstances, the IRS will accept the payment of a smaller sum as payment in full for a larger tax debt. Individual states have similar procedures. If your offer is accepted, tax liens are removed and you are given a fresh start. You should consult with an attorney who specializes in these offers.

Again, the IRS will not approve an installment agreement if you have any tax returns that are not filed so you must make sure first to file all returns that were unfiled.

- All this requires knowledge and (in a perfect world) working with a skilled EA who will fight for you

As mentioned earlier, there are three types of professionals who can represent you before the IRS and negotiate on your behalf and help reach a settlement with the IRS on your case.

Attorney
CPA
Enrolled Agent

The key you want to understand here is the experience of the professional, the types of cases they represent and how successful they are in terms of previous cases. Also do they have an office, staff and support to help them provide you with representation and the other support you will need as a client.

An enrolled agent is a person who has earned the privilege of representing taxpayers before the Internal Revenue Service by either passing a three-part comprehensive IRS test covering individual and business tax returns, or through experience as a former IRS employee. Enrolled agent status is the highest credential the IRS awards. Individuals who obtain this elite status must adhere to ethical standards and complete 72 hours of continuing education courses every three years. Enrolled agents, like attorneys and certified public accountants (CPAs), have unlimited practice rights. This means they are unrestricted as to which taxpayers they can represent, what types of tax matters they can handle, and which IRS offices they can represent clients before. Learn more about enrolled agents in <u>Treasury Department Circular 230</u>

Chapter 8
Never Do These Things

- If you're behind, NEVER "just file" - not without a strategy

If you have unfiled prior year tax returns you want of course to get this resolved. But you want to do this in a manner that does not create more problems for you. Here are some tips and checklist of considerations before you start filing returns.

Never just prepare and file your past due returns
Never file a return without obtaining your IRS transcripts
Never file a return without having all documentation to support the return you file
Never file a past due return without a plan on paying the taxes you will owe
Never prepare and file your own past due return without having a second opinion

These mistakes can lead to more problems after filing because now you are coming back into the tax system trying to get good with Uncle Sam but you have no idea if you have other issues, you are under investigation, or that you may have items reported on your transcripts you forgot about or did not know about.

Simply preparing and filing several past due returns is not a matter of throwing a return together and shoving it into the IRS computer system. You need to map a strategy and look at all possible things that could go wrong and have an action plan ready to deal with those issues if they happen.

Before you prepare the returns

Decide if you want to hire a professional to prepare them or review them after you prepare them
Make sure you include ALL income
Make sure you verify all expenses and deductions
Make sure you have all your records, receipts
Make sure you have all your bank statements
Make sure you order your transcripts from the IRS (Form 4506T)

Filing a late tax return could potentially increase your chances for an IRS audit and then create even more complications for you.

Make sure you understand what options you will have after you file if you owe any tax If possible pay all or as much of the tax as you can when you file. File the oldest year first then work forward for each succeeding year. Make sure you file the late returns with the correct IRS center

You never want to just jump in a file past due returns without taking into account the various other issues you may be left to deal with.

What is your filing strategy, how good are your records, how organized are your receipts, what plan do you have if after filing you owe taxes on the older years. How you will negotiate with the IRS and how you will manage the second stage of your case in the payment of the taxes is equally important.
- *Paradoxically, it's just as bad to not file - not filing is illegal*

Income taxes must be paid on funds above a certain level of income. Regardless of what some theorists may argue, filing taxes is not optional. In fact, failing to file a tax return when you make above a certain amount of money will result in criminal penalties including fines, liens, and even imprisonment. With the Internal Revenue Service being more flexible than ever in helping people pay their tax debt, there is no excuse to avoid filing. In fact, not filing will cost you much more than if you had filed and paid the amount owed.

The Law

According to the Internal Revenue Code, anyone making above the federally established tax exemption limit is required to file a tax return. This includes employees, employers, farmers, military personnel, students, and senior citizens. See IRS Publication 501 which charts the filing requirements for most taxpayers. (There is one major exception to the table. Taxpayers who are still legally the dependents of another person (usually their parents or guardians) must file at smaller levels of income.)

Consequences

The consequences for not filing your taxes snowball as time passes. For instance, delaying your filing past April 15th will automatically result in a fine of either $100 dollars or 5 percent per month of your taxes owed. If you continue refusing to file, the IRS will charge you 100 percent of your taxes owed and will not allow you any deductions or credits. This means that any perks for having dependents, giving to charity, or even paying interest on your mortgage are not considered.

Ignoring bills and notices from the IRS can lead to a determination of tax evasion. Tax evasion is a serious offense that will leave you with a court hearing, marks on your credit, and criminal record. Even worse, if found guilty of tax evasion, you will be fined up to $25,000 dollars and can serve up to 1 year in prison. All this could happen because you did not file your taxes.

Help

If you have earned above the exclusion amount and have not been filing your taxes for whatever reason, the first step should be to prepare tax returns for the years in question, with the help of a tax professional, and then determine the potential amount that you might owe. If the amount is under $25,000 for all of the years combined, then file your tax returns, wait for bills from the IRS showing your total with interest and penalties and then apply for an installment arrangement with the IRS. Doing this helps avoid the potential stigma of tax evasion and shows the IRS that you are making a good faith effort to become compliant.

If the IRS denies you an affordable installment plan, then it is time to consult with a tax expert. An Enrolled Agent for example, can better help you in negotiating with the IRS and making sure that everything is handled in the most expeditious manner and cost effective manner.

If you have not filed a tax return for many years because you had issues in your life that caused you to miss a year or two, and then you buried your head in the sand, it is even more critical that you get those returns prepared and filed as soon as you can. You may find that you actually were due refunds for some or all of the years. A claim for a refund expires after three years, therefore time matters.

- If you've filed but not paid, don't "just pay" - you will 100% pay too much

Again you want to be sure you pay only the legal amount you owe and you want to verify a final amount before paying it and you want to ensure there are no tax lien issues that require additional effort after you pay. It is not uncommon for the IRS to make mistakes, and that your account could have errors that could result in you paying too much or more than you actually owe.

On the other hand you also do not want to play games with filing your past due returns. Tax fraud is a serious problem and could result in serious prison time if convicted. You are already on the radar for not filing, you do not need to add to the problem.

Tax Fraud

Tax fraud is a federal crime with serious consequences and a crime that rarely stays hidden. Between the IRS's audit computers and the Whistleblower program, high dollar tax fraud is nearly impossible to hide. Low dollar tax fraud sometimes can be hidden for a time, but eventually most people get caught.

Filing a fraudulent return can result in fines up to $250,000 for an individual or $500,000 for a corporation and up to 3 years in jail along with the cost of prosecution for high dollar tax fraud. For lower dollar tax fraud you can face penalties of as much as $5000.00 or 100% of the unpaid tax. If the IRS is charging you with high dollar tax fraud, you must hire an attorney and be prepared for a long, difficult and humiliating process.

Keep in mind that the IRS is not out to get responsible taxpayers. In fact, in order to be found guilty of filing a fraudulent tax return the IRS must prove that you: "Willfully makes and subscribes any return, statement, or other document, which contains or is verified by a written declaration that is made under the penalties of perjury, and which he does not believe to be true and correct as to every material matter." (Title 26 USC § 7206(1)) In other words, you must intentionally and knowingly lie on your taxes or other tax related documents. This includes actions such as recurrently leaving certain income off of your tax statements or changing your income forms to reflect false information.

Fraudulent filings: What happens

The first step that the IRS will take when investigating someone for fraud is to pull your tax returns and send you a notice. In the notice, for smaller cases (typically those dealing with amounts less than $100,000), the IRS will request that you address the issues and make repayment immediately. Refusal to do so will result in a formal investigation.

If the amount is larger than $100,000, the IRS's first contact with you will most likely be two IRS agents showing up at your home or office to ask you some questions. If this happens, it is time to hire an attorney. Be polite and respond to the agents by saying that you would prefer to not answer any questions until you retain an attorney. The reason for this is simple: the IRS most likely knows more than you realize and is comparing their records. Any admissions would incriminate you and can result in formal prosecution. Annually, the IRS prosecutes 75 percent of the fraud cases they investigate.

Once you retain an attorney, tell the attorney everything. If you have been fraudulent, the attorney needs to know so that they can mount the right defense. In the case of actually committing fraud, the attorney will do their best to plea bargain your case and mitigate the amount of jail time served. Keep in mind, that if you are found guilty, you name and case will be published on the IRS website and tax fraud will appear on your permanent record. Along with paying a fine and jail time, you will lose your job, business and credibility.

If you have not committed fraud in any way, then bring your paperwork and be prepared to prove this to the attorney. Once the attorney reviews your paperwork, they have the means to obtain the information the IRS has and investigate it for themselves. An attorney can also determine if this was a case of identity fraud or some other mix up. In any event, your attorney will be invaluable in proving your innocence and protecting your record. You have too much to lose if you do not hire a tax professional in a dispute with the IRS.

- Never deal with the IRS directly UNLESS you know all the laws well and are a skilled negotiator

If you are contacted by the IRS you have the right to be represented! Be polite and respectful and tell the IRS Agent you would prefer to hire an attorney or Enrolled Agent before meeting the Agent to discuss their questions. If the IRS agent is a Special Agent you should get an attorney immediately because you are already at the closing end of an investigation and about to have a really bad day.

- Never show off ANY signs of wealth, especially online, if you're behind on your taxes

If you have not filed or paid your taxes do not be a pinhead! Social media, buying luxury cars, fancy vacations, boasting to friends (who could turn you in), all of this is going to come back and smack you in the back side!

Tone it down
Do not show off
Keep records of all income
Keep records of all expenses
Do not play stupid games trying to hide your money off shore! This is a fast ticket to prison.
Do not solicit friends to use their bank to hide your money! Your friend will be in the same cell
Do not play games taking $9500 out of the bank!

Structured financial transactions to avoid the $10,000 cash reporting requirements is a felony and will land you in federal prison

Do not try to launder your money through phantom assets or processing accounts or pre paid debit cards. This is also a form of structuring to avoid reporting or concealing your financial transactions and could look really bad for you in front of a jury.

- Never allow yourself to keep poor records of your expenses, if you can't prove it, you can't write it off, and you're flushing money down the drain

You should immediately set up a record keeping system that allows you to keep all records, receipts and statements of all financial transactions. This is not that difficult and could save you a fortune in lost deductions, audits, or worst case a IRS investigation of tax crimes.

Have one bank account for your business
Do not use it for personal expenses
Keep all statements both online and print them out
Keep all credit card statements

Keep all receipts for all expenses regardless of how you pay for the item

Hire a part time assistant or bookkeeper to help you organize and keep these records

If you pay another person for their services more than $400 issue them a 1099 and file with IRS

Stop listening to people who do not know what they are talking about

Pay for an hour for a tax expert to answer your questions
This could save you tens of thousands of dollars

Chapter 9
The EXACT Steps to Protect Yourself

We will now discuss the exact steps you need to take to protect yourself. If you want to solve your IRS problem there is a good chance much of the work can be done by you but it is also equally important to remember that you are not a tax expert with over 30 years experience in dealing with the IRS. That said if you follow the steps and you take the advice and as long as you are not already under investigation for repeated non filer, chances are pretty good you can work to solve your problem.

It may take you longer doing it yourself but you will save the professional fees you would pay a firm to do all the work for you.

- *First, know your situation and where you stand*

Knowing your situation means;

Are you a non filer for more than 1 year?
Are you a non filer who owes the IRS for more than 1 year?
If after filing your late returns will you owe the IRS?
If so, how much?
Do you have all your IRS account transcripts?
Do you have an IRS Notice or demand for return?
Do you have an IRS Notice or Demand for payment?
Have you been contacted by an IRS Agent?
Have you been contacted by an IRS Special Agent?
How much money have you made for each tax year you have not filed a return for?
How much will you owe in total tax for all years once you file?
Is it more than $50,000?
If it is more than $50,000 do you know you will have to make full financial disclosures to IRS?

Knowing where you stand is critical and you cannot move forward until you have some idea of where you stand and how big the problem is or is not. You really do need to get to that place in your mind where you can stop denial and accept that this must get done and you have no choice but to move forward one tax year at a time.

- Second, gather your records

How many tax years are you dealing with?
Create a checklist of Missing Information Records MIR

All income records
All 1099 and W2
All bank statements
All credit card statements
All merchant statements
All major purchase records, car, house, etc.
All receipts
All stock account records

- Third, learn the laws and become a skilled negotiator BEFORE contacting the IRS (not recommended)...

I never recommend that a taxpayer represent themselves before the IRS. While you can save a lot of money doing much of the work you really do not want to represent yourself before the IRS as you will have a fool for a client. Not knowing the law, the procedure, the Internal Revenue Manual or Regulations can handicap you in so many ways and result in serious consequences or admissions that you may not be required to make.

Preparing the return is not that complicated so long as your income and expenses or business issues are not complicated. When you add buying and selling properties, moving monies around different accounts, not having business records or financial statements you begin to get into an area where you are over your head and should consider professional help in the representation phase if it becomes necessary.

If you do not know.....

Tax rules for deducting travel
Tax rules for deducting meals
Tax rules for deducting entertainment
Tax rules for deducting equipment
Tax rules for reporting income
Tax rules for claiming home office
Tax rules for reporting 1099 expenses

Then you are more likely to have some time you will need to allocate to read the publications and the instructions as you work to prepare your tax returns.

- Or find a skilled enrolled agent to help you (my firm is one option, but there are others--make sure they know what they are doing)

An Enrolled Agent is a highly skilled tax expert in all areas of federal tax law and is authorized to represent you before the IRS in any office or any tax issue in the country. It requires a great deal of experience and education and professional training to attain the credential Enrolled Agent (EA) and of the more than 900,000 tax professionals nationwide there are only 47,000 EA's in the entire country.

You can always look up to locate a local EA in your area. It may be worth the time for an hour consultation to sit down with such an expert to get an idea of what you are up against in your specific case.

- If you are working with an EA, you will get a power of attorney that makes it impossible for the IRS to speak to you directly

An Enrolled Agent is your representative and advocate in resolving matters before the IRS. You will sign IRS Form 2848 Power of Attorney that allows the EA to represent you and requires the IRS to communicate with your representative.

The Enrolled Agent is an expert in all aspects of all federal tax laws including procedure and representation. The EA is the professional who will know how to guide you through the process in reaching a settlement with the IRS to file all past due returns and hold collection enforcement to give you time to determine your correct liability and make arrangements for an installment agreement, an offer in compromise or perhaps a hardship order.

- That individual and his team will submit documentation to the IRS and get a grace period that stops enforcement while they are working on your returns

For a case where there are numerous prior year returns that need to be filed it is a bit of a work load to be sure. The EA will negotiate with the IRS in many cases to stop collection and other enforcement against you while time is provided to prepare and file all past due returns.

Important in this process is to not delay the time to resolve you case. The IRS has strict rules that prohibit taking actions to intentionally delay or frustrate the IRS in the administration of the tax laws. This grace period if you will is designed to give the EA time granted by the IRS on your behalf in order to do all the necessary research, find out from the IRS if there are other issues that require attention, and to come to an agreement as to the time IRS will allow to bring all returns into compliance and file with the IRS.

- Once your returns are filed, you are no longer in non-compliance status; once your tax bill amount has been established, or if you've filed but not paid, the enrolled agent will typically be negotiating your offer in compromise or the terms of your payment plan with the IRS

These negotiations are critical to ensure all matters are closed successfully and that the IRS has everything they require to reflect you are now in full compliance. Of course you can negotiate for your own case but again if you are not familiar with the process, procedures, the rules and the law and are not trained in asserting your rights, your appeal and hearing rights you could potentially miss an important issue that could result in more difficulty for you later.

You want to ensure the case is closed
You want to ensure all returns are accepted
You want to ensure all returns post to your master file account
You want to ensure the assessment notice is correct once the IRS sends you the bill
You want to make sure if it is not you appeal the assessment
You want to ensure the IRS no longer shows you in non-filer status as non-compliant
You want to ensure the terms of making any payment agreement allow all considerations for you

- Remember, depending on your situation, how you do this can make the difference in you overpaying tens of thousands of dollars, massive penalties, higher than you can afford payments that cripple your life

The art and skill of negotiating with the IRS and using all your rights and the law in your favor is something that takes many years of study and doing it every day for hundreds of taxpayers each year. You want to have a professional at this level in some cases representing you to ensure you are following the rules but also to make sure the IRS is also following the rules and not abusing your rights or taking advantage of your lack of knowledge or skill.

- A tale of three tax payers: one didn't do this right, and went to jail...another filed but did it on their own, and paid a fortune... the third person followed this advice and paid pennies on the dollar

Case Study 1
A taxpayer some years back was issued an IRS notice and refused to respond. Sometime later he visited my offices and we discussed the case and he decided to have me represent him. Later when the Agent demanded to see certain records he refused to provide them. The Agent then issued a summons for which the client refused to provide the information a second time. By this time I disengaged

representation of the client, he was arrested and brought before a federal magistrate and again refused to abide by the summons. He was immediately incarcerated for contempt of court and spent 11 months in jail until he finally decided to provide the materials under the summons. He lost his business, his wife divorced him and it took years for him to recover financially.

Case Study 2
A taxpayer had not filed corporate or personal returns for 8 years. He hired his dad, a retired CPA to initially represent him to deal with the matter himself. This went south very fast and the IRS expanded the examination. By the time I was retained in the case, the client was looking at a total of $889,000 in taxes, interest and penalties. Some 15 months later I negotiated with the IRS and the entire case settled for slightly over $410,000. However had the client followed even basic advice and set up his business and taxes according to a managed plan he would have saved another $200,000 in cost.

Case Study 3
The client had not filed tax returns for 9 years. He was anxious, stressed and even having medical issues due to the worry. He was convinced that he would owe a few hundred thousand dollars to the IRS plus penalties. He hired my firm and we were able to reconstruct all the returns and the financial information and when it was finally over in late 2015 we settled the case with the IRS for about $21,000 total.

- *Which person do you want to be?*

Do it yourself, ignore it, or get it done with the assistance of a qualified professional who knows every aspect of tax law and who will fight to protect your rights in representing you before the IRS. You want to close your case and never deal with it again so you must decide how you want to proceed.

Much of the case work for smaller cases can be done by you and you may want only to have a professional review the work.

Whatever you decide you will do, at least make the decision to begin resolving your issues with the IRS before you wind up financially upside down and in serious trouble with the IRS.

Chapter 10
What's Next for YOU?

- Hopefully, you now have a complete understanding of your problem and why you can't delay

My hope is that this material has helped you to understand how to define your problem, map a solution and educate you so that in the case where you may hire a professional you at least know the questions to ask and will not be taken advantage of by fly by night so-called tax resolution firms only after your money.

The longer you wait of course the higher the risk that a small or medium problem will escalate into a major problem and then the costs become untenable in professional fees. I would rather have a client pay me a fee to manage their taxes than to solve their tax problem. It is far lest costly and more enjoyable than dealing with IRS agents all day who are trying to take everything away from the client.

- This is a HUGE first step-but it's also just that--a first step

Yes this is just a first step.

You must take the next step and decide how to go about solving your problem. Interestingly even in a DIY situation you can hire a firm like my firm to help guide you in the DIY solution. You save money on professional fees, you learn more about your taxes and yes you begin to solve your problem getting it squared away with the IRS.

Are you a non filer?
You have not filed or paid
Are you a delinquent account?
You filed but have not paid

What is your first next step?
Organize your records
Obtain your transcripts
Seek a second opinion for assistance in DIY solution

Whatever you decide congratulations for deciding to finally resolve your IRS problems and take the lead before you have to encounter and meet an IRS Agent, Revenue Officer or Special Agent. You do not want the stress that this can bring into our business and your life.

- Much more is needed and what you do will depend on many factors like your years not filed, how much you potentially owe, your budget, time and more

I believe the most important step has begin by your gaining new awareness and willing to take a next step in solving your IRS problems. You do need to take an inventory and assessment of your problem, define it and map out what your options are.

You have rights under the law and so long as you are making an honest effort to solve your problem, you can within reason expect that even the IRS will be willing to assist you in a final resolution. After all the IRS wants you to file and pay your taxes.

When you go more than 2 years not filing then it starts to seem like a problem so big it just cannot be solved or you do not know how or where to begin.

This book is designed to give you all the knowledge and information you need to define your problem and educate you about the process and your many options. Having represented clients for many years before the IRS I can tell you that today is more challenging than I have ever seen or experienced. Partly due to the political climate which should not matter, and partly due to the attitude of a small handful of IRS agents that fail to respect the fact that you have rights regardless of the underlying situation.

- The most important thing is that you take informed ACTION - and if you get help - with the right individual or team who will do things properly

DO not discount the value of a DIY solution

We often coach many clients every day on how to solve a problem, or how to take a next step to solving a problem.

You have many advantages as I have stated in that if you begin the solution first before the IRS contacts you it will always give you the advantage in reaching a final solution.

The process is not complicated

Determine your problem; non file or non payment
Determine the number of years at issue
Assess the volume of records you have against what you will need
Determine how much time each day you will allocate to working on and solving your problem
Map out a check list of action steps to take
Map out a resource list of resources you need and those you have
Set realistic goals to accomplish each task
Break down the process into simple tasks that are easy to reach
Then execute
Do something each day toward solving your problem

Develop stronger relationship with your money
Work to understand your taxes
Try to understand what it was that caused you to defer dealing with the problem to begin with
Work to improve on creating better money habits

All of these will help you on the path to financial success and freedom.

- We offer advanced education and coaching, list the resources

- And of course, we offer services described - though with the success of this book there is now a waiting list

You can obtain some personal coaching toward helping you solve the problem

Currently due to popular demand there is a waiting list
We can provide a short 20 minute consultation
We can offer a review of your work
We can even assist you in making sure the process is followed correctly

Representation means we take responsibility to deal with the IRS on your behalf but we can arrange it where you can do much of the work if you prefer and we can review that thus saving you in professional fees.

- Again, we do not recommend dealing directly with the IRS, but if you must or have zero budget at all, then learn the laws well, be meticulous with your numbers/records and take a negotiating class or book first

The problem is that if you do not know what your rights are or what the law requires you could end up creating more problems.

You may wish to hire our firm to resolve the entire case for you

Here are some benefits

Experts in all aspects of federal and state tax law
Admitted to practice before the IRS
Discounted fees as a member of our coaching program
We will even finance your fee engagement with the firm and create an easy pay plan for you
We have the staff to perform part of the work and allow you to save money and do part yourself

Everything in reason is negotiable

The most important point is we truly want to help you begin solving the problem and not get taken advantage of working with one of those marketing firms who will take your case, charge you $20,000 and then try to sell your case file to someone like me!

- List of other recommended service providers

To find an Enrolled Agent go to

www.NAEA.Org
Search for FIND AN ENROLLED AGENT

- Our programs and services page
www.StopMyIRSBill.com

ABOUT THE AUTHOR

James Harnsberger is an Enrolled Agent admitted to practice before the IRS and has been a tax expert for over 30 years. A credentialed paralegal, and NTPI Fellow, James is a passionate practitioner for taxpayers and business owners especially. One of his greatest desires is to bring about more strength in the Taxpayer Bill of Rights and to work to end abuses by the IRS.

Made in the USA
San Bernardino, CA
27 August 2017